OUR DAILY BREAD
FOR
KIDS®
JUMBO
Bible Activity & Coloring Book

Crystal Bowman & Teri McKinley

Our Daily Bread
Publishing.

Our Daily Bread for Kids: Jumbo Bible Activity & Coloring Book
© 2021 by Our Daily Bread Publishing

Illustrations by Luke Flowers
© 2016, 2018, 2021 by Our Daily Bread Publishing

All rights reserved.

This book is compiled from portions of
Our Daily Bread for Kids Bible Quizzes & Games (3 volumes, © 2017, 2018, 2019)
and *Our Daily Bread for Kids Coloring & Activity Books* (3 volumes, © 2015, 2018, 2020).

Requests for permission to quote from this book should be directed to:
Permissions Department, Our Daily Bread Publishing, PO Box 3566, Grand Rapids, MI 49501,
or contact us by email at permissionsdept@odb.org.

Quiz questions and answers, unless otherwise indicated, are based on the Holy Bible,
New International Version®, NIV®. Copyright © 1973, 1978, 1984, 2011 by Biblica, Inc.™
Used by permission of Zondervan. All rights reserved worldwide. www.zondervan.com.

Scripture quotations marked NKJV are from the New King James Version®. Copyright © 1982 by Thomas Nelson.
Used by permission. All rights reserved.

Scripture quotations marked NIrV are taken from the Holy Bible,
New International Reader's Version®, NIrV®. Copyright © 1995, 1996, 1998, 2014 by Biblica, Inc.™
Used by permission of Zondervan. All rights reserved worldwide. www.zondervan.com.

Interior design by Kris Nelson/StoryLook Design

ISBN: 978-1-64070-109-0

Printed in the United States of America
24 25 26 27 28 29 30 / 9 8 7 6 5 4 3

Know Your Bible

Many different people wrote down the books of the Bible, but God is the real author. His Holy Spirit guided all the Bible writers. God used people to write the words, but He told each one what to say.

WHAT DO YOU KNOW ABOUT THE BIBLE?

1. **Who wrote the first 5 books of the Bible?** (Deuteronomy 31:24)

   a) Adam
   b) Abraham
   c) Moses
   d) Jacob

2. **Who wrote many of the other Old Testament books?** (Hebrews 1:1)

   a) prophets
   b) shepherds
   c) judges
   d) doctors

3. **How many books are in the Old Testament?** (See table of contents in your Bible)

   a) 24
   b) 39
   c) 35
   d) 47

4. **Why were many of the Psalms written?** (Psalm 95:1–2)

   a) to teach kids how to read
   b) to learn about shepherds
   c) for praising God and singing
   d) for bedtime stories

5. **What exciting story is found in Luke chapter 2?**

   a) the crossing of the Red Sea
   b) the birth of Jesus
   c) Daniel in the lions' den
   d) David and Goliath

6. **Why was the book of John written?** (John 20:31)

   a) the author liked to tell stories
   b) the author wanted to be famous
   c) to show people what good writing is
   d) so people would believe in Jesus

7. **How many books are in the New Testament?** (See table of contents in your Bible)

   a) 12
   b) 20
   c) 27
   d) 66

8. **Who wrote many of the books in the New Testament?** (Romans 1:1)

   a) Jonah
   b) Lazarus
   c) Zacchaeus
   d) the apostle Paul

Find the answers on page 173

Word Search

Can you find all the words?
Words may be forward, up-and-down, or diagonal.

AUTHOR   GOD   PAUL

BIBLE   JESUS   PROPHETS

BOOKS   LUKE   PSALMS

DISCIPLES   MOSES   TESTAMENT

```
W Y M T C R D I S C I P L E S M W V H Q
X M W M P D R T I K P T N L U K E C Y P
Y Q M D O M T X I R L T I M O R F Q R J
B C W M P S X B T V T L I N V C R W S E
I W X Q Z B E L P C V V T S B R Y P M S
B F K B W Q D S Q D S Z R U Q O L L I U
L K X M B D B P P K C G V G O D L T T S
E F R H D M N T T J B B D M L O Q X L R
L K T M B A U T H O R K L N M P B D R H
K T B Q N J W M H R B S N B Q M B X S F
W T E S T A M E N T W L T N P X K H C P
M P R O P H E T S M M N X T L T P N D A
Q T K N W S T Q P S A L M S D C H F Q U
K X V F M G D B K L R T S M B O O K S L
```

Find the answers on page 173

4

Make as many words as you can out of the letters in

Old Testament

_____   _____

_____   _____

_____   _____

_____   _____

_____   _____

_____   _____

_____   _____

_____   _____

_____   _____

Word Art

Color the letters and words about some of the books in the Old Testament: Pentateuch, Historical, and Wisdom.

The total number of books in the Old Testament is _____.

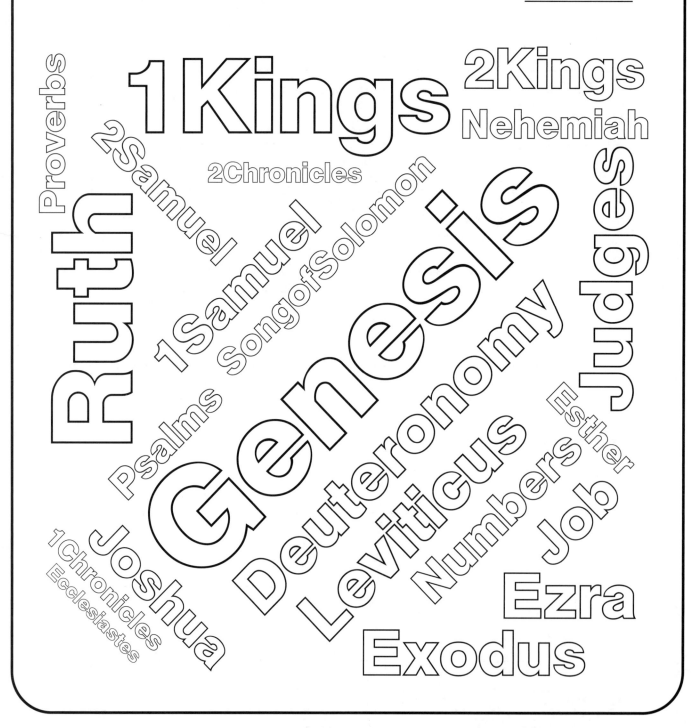

Find the answers on page 174

God said, "Let the _____ under
the sky be gathered into one place.
Let_____ ground appear."
And that's exactly what happened.

Genesis 1:9 NIrV

A Special Creation

In the beginning, there was nothing but water and darkness. The earth was empty. It had no shape. But God was there before everything else, and He had a plan to create a world.

WHAT DO YOU KNOW ABOUT THE STORY OF CREATION?

1. According to Genesis 1:1, when did God create "the heavens and the earth"?

   a) billions of years ago
   b) 4000 BC
   c) in the beginning
   d) when the time was right

2. What does the Bible say the brand-new earth was like? (Genesis 1:2)

   a) bright and cheerful
   b) formless and empty
   c) sticky and gooey
   d) loud and busy

3. How many days did God use to fill and complete His heavens and earth? (Genesis 1:31)

   a) one
   b) two
   c) six
   d) twenty-one

4. What did God think of His work after each day of creation?
   (Genesis 1:4, 10, 12, 18, 21, 25, 31)

   a) it was cool
   b) it was right
   c) it was amazing
   d) it was good

5. What was the first thing God put on the earth's dry ground?
   (Genesis 1:11–12)

   a) human beings
   b) plants and trees
   c) animals and birds
   d) swings and teeter-totters

6. How does the Bible say God brought most of creation into being? (Genesis 1:3, 6, 9, 11, 14, 20, 24)

   a) He spoke
   b) He thought really hard
   c) He snapped His finger
   d) He waved His hand

7. The first human was made differently. What did God use to create Adam? (Genesis 2:7)

   a) animal bones
   b) tree sap
   c) clouds and rain
   d) dust of the earth

8. What place did God make as a home for Adam and his wife, Eve?
   (Genesis 2:15)

   a) the Mount of Olives
   b) the Pool of Siloam
   c) the Garden of Eden
   d) the Valley of Elah

Find the answers on page 174

Crossword Puzzle

ACROSS

3. Another name for our world (Genesis 1:1)
4. What name did God give to the darkness? (Genesis 1:5)
5. The name of the first woman (Genesis 3:20)
7. God made fish to live in the _____ (Genesis 1:21)
8. Besides human beings, what did God make on the sixth day? (Genesis 1:25)
10. To make something out of nothing (Genesis 1:1)
11. Who made everything? (Genesis 1:1)

DOWN

1. Another name for sky (Genesis 1:1)
2. In what book of the Bible can you read the story of creation?
6. The name of the garden God created (Genesis 2:8)
8. What name did God give to the first man? (Genesis 2:20)
9. What did God create on the first day? (Genesis 1:3)

Word Search

Can you find all the words?
Words may be forward or up-and-down.

ANIMALS	LIGHT	STARS
BIRDS	MOON	SUN
GARDEN	PEOPLE	TREES
GOOD	PLANTS	WATER

```
E C P K L S R B P N
S Q P E O P L E M N X Z
G O O D P M S S T A R S D L
R T Q C T M Q B C S N S M T T H
Y T W F T G A R D E N P X M R R T M
T P L C X A N I M A L S X W E Q V T
K N L G T D M O O N T R L T E X Z R
W A T E R Q H G N M P L K W S F X C
T C X L M P L A N T S T B B W T R Y
R T L I G H T S D C T I I Z X S
T N Q V X Z S Q D T R R K D
F G B H H U T Y L P D C
O B N H N Z H B D S
```

Find the answers on page 174

The First Family

The Bible begins with the book of Genesis, which tells how God created a very good and beautiful world. In Genesis, we also learn about Adam and Eve, the first people who lived on earth. They had many children, grandchildren, and great-grandchildren.

WHAT DO YOU KNOW ABOUT THE VERY FIRST PEOPLE?

1. **What did Adam and Eve do that messed up the world God made?** (Genesis 3:6)

   a) they didn't take care of the animals
   b) they forgot to water the garden
   c) they picked the flowers
   d) they ate some fruit that God told them not to eat

2. **What kind of work did Cain, the first child born on earth, do?** (Genesis 4:2)

   a) he was a farmer
   b) he was a shepherd
   c) he made tents
   d) he fixed computers

3. **What kind of work did Cain's younger brother, Abel, do?** (Genesis 4:2)

   a) he made pottery
   b) he was a shepherd
   c) he was a hunter
   d) he was a writer

4. **What happened that made Cain angry?** (Genesis 4:4–5)

   a) his plants wilted in the sun
   b) birds ate his fruit
   c) God was not pleased with his offering
   d) his brother took some of his vegetables

5. **What did Cain do because of his anger?** (Genesis 4:8)

   a) he ran away from home
   b) he stole Abel's sheep
   c) he killed his brother, Abel
   d) he burned his garden

6. **What was the name of Adam and Eve's third son, born after Abel?** (Genesis 5:3)

   a) Joshua
   b) Benjamin
   c) Samuel
   d) Seth

7. **What happened to Enoch, a descendant of Adam who loved God?** (Genesis 5:24)

   a) he became a ruler
   b) he became sick and died
   c) God took him up to heaven
   d) he became rich and famous

8. **Enoch's son Methuselah lived longer than any other person. How many birthdays did he have?** (Genesis 5:27)

   a) 580
   b) 650
   c) 789
   d) 969

Find the answers on page 174

God was sad when Adam and Eve did not obey Him.
But He still loved them.

Crossword Puzzle

ACROSS

2. Someone who grows fruits and vegetables
5. God's home
7. The name of the first woman (Genesis 3:20)
8. The oldest man who ever lived (Genesis 5:27)
11. The first child ever born (Genesis 4:1)
12. God created the whole _____ for us to enjoy

DOWN

1. The first family had many _____
3. The second son born into the first family (Genesis 4:2)
4. A person who takes care of sheep
6. He walked and talked with God (Genesis 5:22)
9. The son born after Abel died (Genesis 5:3)
10. The name of the first man (Genesis 3:20)

Find the answers on page 175

Color by Number

Can you find the hidden picture?

1 = Brown   2 = Green   3 = Blue   4 = Yellow   5 = Purple   6 = Red

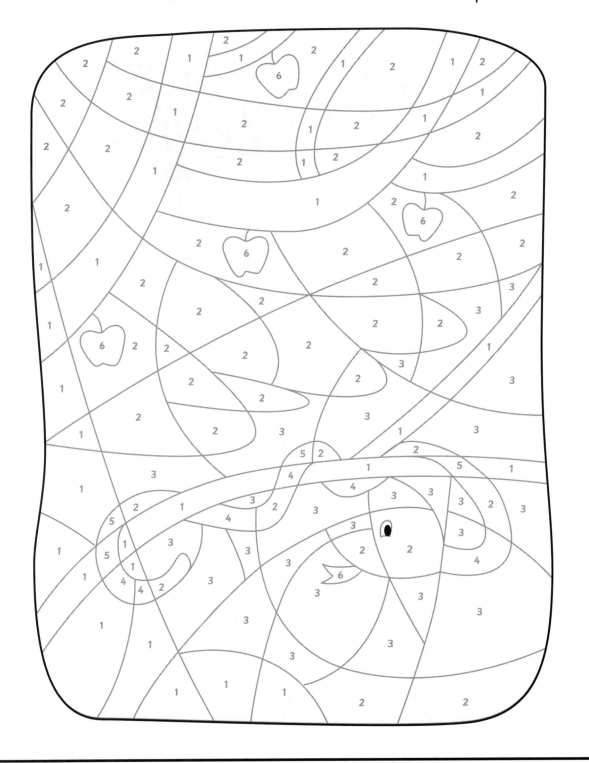

14

Word Search

Can you find all the words? Words may be
forward or backward, up-and-down, or diagonal.

ADAM	EVE	HIDE
BITE	FORGIVENESS	SNAKE
CLOTHES	FRUIT	TEMPTATION
DISOBEY	GARDEN	TREE

```
G A D M A S D F K L P O C L O T H E S
A N O I H W A B N I W E B T S E M O I
R F S S E N E V I G R O F L A B S T K
D A N L N S W E L T L Y J E T D H O T
E L A E H L T I N S E L E O W I A H U
N M K Y I D R Y E A L O D M H S U M H
L T E M P T A T I O N M A S T O E D S
E M N I E K M R L V G C U N M B T H A
S O W L H I D E U F I T N E V E D E R
I T H M U A S E B R C K A W I Y B A O
A O S N C E I H A F R U I T V E H O N
```

Find the answers on page 175

Word Art

Color the letters and words about the first family.

The story of the first family can be found in the Bible in the book of _____.

Find the answers on page 175

Make as many words as you can out of the letters in

Methuselah

_____   _____

_____   _____

_____   _____

_____   _____

_____   _____

_____   _____

_____   _____

_____   _____

Find the Match

Draw a line between the arks that are exactly alike.

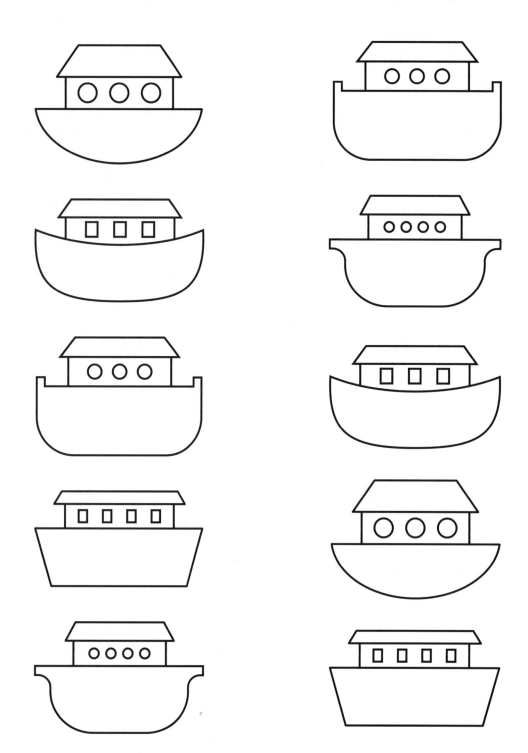

Find the answers on page 175

Noah, Abraham, & Joseph

The Bible is filled with many exciting stories about people who loved God. Sometimes they had to do things that were hard. But because they loved God, they did what He wanted them to do.

WHAT DO YOU KNOW ABOUT NOAH, ABRAHAM, AND JOSEPH?

1. **According to Genesis 6:14, what did God tell Noah to do?**
   a) build a raft
   b) build a bridge
   c) build an ark
   d) take swimming lessons

2. **Why did God want to send a flood to cover the earth?** (Genesis 6:5)
   a) the people were very sinful
   b) the trees needed water
   c) the fish needed more room to swim
   d) Noah had prayed for rain

3. **How long did it rain after Noah and his family went inside the ark?** (Genesis 7:12)
   a) two years
   b) four months
   c) twenty-five weeks
   d) forty days and forty nights

4. **According to Genesis 12:1, what did God tell Abram to do?**
   a) go on vacation
   b) get a job
   c) get married
   d) leave his country and his family

5. **What promise did God make to Abram?** (see Genesis 12:2)
   a) his wife would have twins
   b) he would be a king
   c) his family would become a great nation
   d) he would live for 300 years

6. **What new name did God give to Abram?** (Genesis 17:5)
   a) Abe
   b) Abraham
   c) Isaac
   d) Israel

7. **What did Joseph's brothers do to him?** (Genesis 37:28)
   a) they made a pretty coat for him
   b) they gave him a crown to wear
   c) they sold him as a slave
   d) they hid him in a cave

8. **How did God use Joseph?** (Genesis 41:41)
   a) Joseph built a big city
   b) Joseph became an important ruler in Egypt
   c) Joseph fought wild animals
   d) Joseph taught people how to make bricks

Find the answers on page 175

God said to Noah, "The _____ is the sign of my covenant. I have made my covenant between me and all life on earth."

Genesis 9:17 NIrV

Word Search

Can you find all the words?
Words may be forward, backward, or up-and-down.

NOAH	ABRAHAM	FLOOD
SARAH	ARK	JAPHETH
OLD	HAM	PROMISE
SHEM	ISAAC	NAME

H D S M N O A H K L O S H
M E H S C G M S C D G R A
F L O O D H T G H K D E M
M B N B M E W D J A P H E T H Q W K B X Z
A R Q K M W B P R O M I S E K B R D L O H
R H D G R T I S A A C B N M S C S A R A H
K B D Q D L L P A B R A H A M T P L X N T
K H G N N A M E T K L P G H R T K F G R E

Find the answers on page 176

Crossword Puzzle

ACROSS

3. The first book of the Bible
5. Noah had three _____ (Genesis 6:10)
7. Abram's new name (Genesis 17:5)
9. The opposite of young
11. The name of Abraham's wife (Genesis 17:15)
12. Another word for trust (Acts 16:31)

DOWN

1. God sent the flood because the people were _____
2. Whom did God see as a righteous man? (Genesis 6:9)
4. The name of Abraham and Sarah's son (Genesis 21:3)
6. God made a _____ to Abraham
8. God told Noah to bring animals into the _____ (Genesis 7:1–2)
10. One of Noah's sons (Genesis 6:10)

Find the answers on page 176

God said to Abraham, "Go from your _____, your people, and your father's_____. Go to the land I will show you."

Genesis 12:1 NIrV

Word Search

Can you find all the words?
Words may be forward, backward, or up-and-down.

ABRAHAM	GENESIS	PROMISE
ARK	JOSEPH	RAIN
EGYPT	NATION	RULER
FLOOD	NOAH	SLAVE

H G T L S L A V E D V B C W A X S B M Q F

L D G B V C X Z W N A T I O N M B W Q G L

C H R R E B N M K P C Q W R T Y P M K G O

N B U V D N A T P C N M H B K L P K W B O

O X L D W Q S T M T P Y G E D W S Z Q R D

A F E T H W M Q B A R K T H G D S W Q S T

H G R B B Q V W N R Q G H G E N E S I S M

Y R T H G D C B M J O S E P H W G H M Q L

S G H K L A B R A H A M M R H P N I A R B

S P R B R H P R O M I S E Q T B T H L N T

Find the answers on page 176

The Chosen People

God kept His promise to Abraham by giving him a son. Abraham was about a hundred years old and his wife, Sarah, was around ninety! God's promise to Abraham continued through Isaac's family after he got married and had two sons. Isaac's sons were very different from each other and didn't get along well.

WHAT DO YOU KNOW ABOUT ISAAC AND HIS FAMILY?

1. **How did God test Abraham's obedience in the land of Moriah?** (Genesis 22:2)

   a) He told Abraham to jump into the Dead Sea
   b) He told Abraham to write Genesis
   c) He told Abraham to marry Hagar
   d) He told Abraham to sacrifice his son

2. **Who did Isaac marry?** (Genesis 24:51)

   a) Rachel
   b) Rebekah
   c) Ruth
   d) Rahab

3. **What were the names of Isaac's twin sons?** (Genesis 25:25–26)

   a) David and Jonathan
   b) Ham and Shem
   c) James and John
   d) Jacob and Esau

4. **How did Jacob trick his father into blessing him?** (Genesis 27:18–19)

   a) he pretended to be his brother, Esau
   b) he switched the lambs of his father's flock with the lambs of his uncle's flock
   c) he asked for his father's blessing while his father was sleeping
   d) he gave his father an expensive gift

5. **Who did Jacob live with when he ran away from Esau?** (Genesis 28:5)

   a) the king
   b) a friend
   c) his grandfather
   d) an uncle

6. **What did God promise Jacob when he left home?** (Genesis 28:13)

   a) he would lead God's people out of Egypt
   b) he would receive a special land for his family
   c) he would have twelve sons
   d) he would become a great prophet

7. **What kind of animals did Jacob's uncle Laban raise?** (Genesis 29:9–10)

   a) cows
   b) pigs
   c) sheep
   d) chickens

8. **What was the name of Laban's daughter who Jacob met at a well?** (Genesis 29:10)

   a) Leah
   b) Deborah
   c) Rachel
   d) Miriam

Find the answers on page 176

Spot the Difference

Circle the one sheep that is
different from the rest of the flock.

Find the answers on page 177

Jacob and Esau were Isaac's sons.
They were twins, but they did not look alike.

Crossword Puzzle

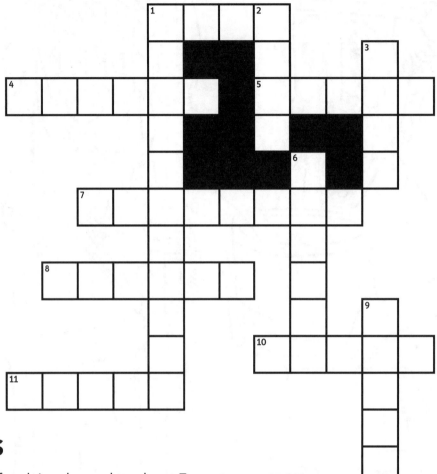

ACROSS

1. The food Jacob used to cheat Esau (Genesis 25:29)
4. The name Jacob gave the place where he built a pillar to God (Genesis 28:18–19)
5. The name of Jacob's uncle (Genesis 24:29)
7. Jacob stole Esau's _____ (Genesis 27:30–31)
8. Jacob's uncle lived in _____ Aram (Genesis 28:2)
10. Rebekah's husband (Genesis 24:67)
11. Jacob and Esau were _____ (Genesis 25:24–26)

DOWN

1. Rachel's job (Genesis 29:9 NKJV)
2. The place where Jacob met Rachel (Genesis 29:10)
3. God promised to give ____ to Jacob's family (Genesis 28:13)
6. What Jacob saw going up and down a ladder in his dream (Genesis 28:12)
9. Esau's body was very _____ (Genesis 25:25)

Find the answers on page 177

Jacob Gets Married

God's promise to Abraham continued through Jacob, who was Abraham's grandson. Jacob agreed to work for seven years so he could marry his Uncle Laban's daughter Rachel, whom he loved very much. But Laban tricked Jacob.

WHAT DO YOU KNOW JACOB AND HIS FAMILY?

1. **What was the trick that Laban played on Jacob?** (Genesis 29:25)

   a) he fooled Jacob into marrying Rachel's sister, Leah

   b) he made Jacob pay 30 pieces of silver

   c) he told Jacob Rachel was sick

   d) he sent Rachel away

2. **What happened to Rachel?** (Genesis 29:26–28)

   a) she became Leah's servant

   b) she married the king of the land

   c) she became Jacob's second wife

   d) she moved to China

3. **What new name did God give Jacob?** (Genesis 32:28)

   a) Isaac

   b) Isaiah

   c) Ishmael

   d) Israel

4. **How many sons did Jacob have?** (Genesis 35:23–26)

   a) 7

   b) 10

   c) 12

   d) 13

5. **What were the names of Rachel's two sons?** (Genesis 35:24)

   a) Judah and Manasseh

   b) Joseph and Benjamin

   c) Levi and Simeon

   d) Issachar and Reuben

6. **Why didn't Joseph's brothers like him?** (Genesis 37:4)

   a) he stole their sheep

   b) he ate their dinner

   c) their father liked Joseph the best

   d) their sisters were nice to Joseph

7. **What did Joseph's brothers do to him?** (Genesis 37:25–27)

   a) they stole his sandals

   b) they sold him as a slave

   c) they took his lunch

   d) they shaved his head

8. **What happened when Joseph was in Egypt?** (Genesis 41:40)

   a) he was forced to build the pyramids

   b) he led God's people out of the land

   c) he became the second most important leader

   d) he was in prison for the rest of his life

Find the answers on page 177

Joseph's brothers were jealous and sold him as a slave.
He became a great ruler in Egypt.

Color by Number

Color Joseph's robe using the key below.

1 = Red   3 = Green   5 = Yellow   7 = Pink

2 = Blue   4 = Orange   6 = Purple   8 = Black

Word Search

Can you find all the words?
Words may be forward, backward, or up-and-down.

JOSEPH	PRISON	STARS
TWELVE	WIFE	REUBEN
ROBE	ISRAEL	LEAH
DREAM	BROTHERS	BENJAMIN

```
      A J V W K L E R G D
    Q S U Y L C M I H R S P
    S R T H G K L P T N B T S Q
    S R A T S G R N B E N J A M I N
  F N T L T W E L V E W F H A E L T P
  D R E B T R E U B E N S M Q M E T N T B
  G O T R D R E A M L T J N N D H N J W C
  Q B R O T H E R S H L T V S W B K L I W
  B E K L H P E S O J M W N T K N L S F R
  M P R I S O N T N N S R D H D N K E
  R S R K B I S R A E L W R P K M
  R R Y T J H F J T L B W N S
    T M U I L Z U Q M G A B
    V R A C B H Y F K O
```

The Israelites Go To Egypt

A famine sent Jacob's sons to Egypt, where they were very surprised to meet Joseph! He forgave his brothers for selling him as a slave, and soon the whole family moved to Egypt. The descendants of Abraham, Isaac, and Jacob were called the Israelites.

WHAT DO YOU KNOW ABOUT ABOUT THE ISRAELITES IN EGYPT?

1. **What did Joseph tell his brothers after their father, Jacob, died?** (Genesis 50:21)

   a) he would send them back home

   b) he would put them in prison

   c) he would provide for them and their children

   d) he would teach them how to make pyramids

2. **As time went on after Joseph died, what happened to the Israelites?** (Exodus 1:9)

   a) they played too many video games

   b) they moved to Assyria

   c) they grew in number

   d) they invented writing

3. **What did the new Egyptian king, the Pharaoh, do to the Israelites?** (Exodus 1:14)

   a) he gave them food and sent them back to Canaan

   b) he treated them badly and made them work very hard

   c) he teased them and called them bad names

   d) he made them eat frogs and lizards

4. **What did God tell Moses to do?** (Exodus 3:10)

   a) become the next Pharaoh of Egypt

   b) build houses for the Israelites

   c) bring the Israelites out of Egypt

   d) climb a pyramid

5. **After God sent ten plagues and Pharaoh finally let the Israelites leave Egypt, what body of water did they have to cross?** (Exodus 13:18)

   a) the Dead Sea

   b) the Black Sea

   c) the Red Sea

   d) the Deep Blue Sea

6. **At the sea, what did God tell Moses to do?** (Exodus 14:15–16)

   a) get into a big boat

   b) start swimming

   c) scream and shout

   d) hold his staff over the sea to divide the water

7. **What was the first of the Ten Commandments God gave to Moses and the Israelites during their wilderness wandering?** (Exodus 20:1–17)

   a) "You shall not talk in the library"

   b) "You shall have no other gods before me"

   c) "You shall not murder"

   d) "Honor your father and your mother"

8. **Who became the leader of the Israelites after Moses?** (Deuteronomy 34:9)

   a) Benjamin

   b) Caleb

   c) Joshua

   d) Judah

Find the answers on page 178

God spoke to Moses from the burning bush,
"Go to Egypt and free my people!"

Make as many words as you can out of the letters in

Miracle

_____   _____

_____   _____

_____   _____

_____   _____

_____   _____

_____   _____

_____   _____

_____   _____

_____   _____

God parted the waters of the Red Sea
so Moses could lead the Israelites safely across.

Crossword Puzzle

ACROSS

2. The name of Joseph's father (Genesis 46:19)

3. What moms and dads have

6. The people walked through the sea on _____ ground (Exodus 14:22)

7. The country where Potiphar bought Joseph as a slave (Genesis 39:1)

10. The Israelites lived in the wilderness for forty _____ (Joshua 5:6)

11. Who led the Israelites out of Egypt? (Exodus 14:1–4)

DOWN

1. The Egyptians made the Israelites _____ very hard (Exodus 1:14)

2. The name of Rachel's oldest son (Genesis 35:24)

4. The name that was given to Abraham, Isaac, and Jacob's descendants (Exodus 1:7)

5. What the Israelites had to cross after leaving Egypt (Exodus 13:18)

8. The name given to the king of Egypt (Genesis 39:1)

9. How many commandments did God give to Moses? (Exodus 20:1–17)

Find the answers on page 178

Word Search

Can you find all the words?
Words may be forward, backward, or diagonal.

PHARAOH   JOSEPH   JACOB

WILDERNESS   MOSES   ISRAELITES

EGYPTIANS   RED SEA   FORTY

COMMANDMENTS   EXODUS   LEADER

```
K H M J Q Z C O M M A N D M E N T S
B O C A J M W N H F O R T Y N H G T
S G F H R M W Q R E D S E A Q R B T
H P E S O J S M T D T R E D A E L M
P Q N K P H A R A O H T S S B X N H
S D I S R A E L I T E S D W F S M Q
H E G Y P T I A N S N Q E X O D U S
C H R W I L D E R N E S S M H N O Q
```

Find the answers on page 178

More Israelite Leaders

After Moses died, God used other men and women to lead His people. Joshua led the Israelites across the Jordan River into the land God promised them. Later, God gave other people important jobs as judges, a word which can mean "deliverer."

WHAT DO YOU KNOW ABOUT SOME OF ISRAEL'S LEADERS?

1. **What did God tell the priests to do at the Jordan River?** (Joshua 3:8)

   a) strike the water with their staffs
   b) stand still in the middle of the river with the ark of the covenant
   c) take off their sandals
   d) throw out their fishing nets

2. **Who went to see Joshua before he went into battle?** (Joshua 5:13–14)

   a) Moses
   b) Jacob's twelve sons
   c) his older brothers
   d) the commander of the Lord's army

3. **What did Joshua and the Israelites do to bring down the wall around Jericho?** (Joshua 6:15, 20)

   a) they fired cannon balls
   b) they knocked it down one stone at a time
   c) they marched around the city seven times, blew trumpets, and shouted
   d) they poured olive oil over it

4. **Why did the Israelites go to see Deborah?** (Judges 4:4–5)

   a) she sold clothing
   b) she made bread
   c) she taught the people how to sing
   d) she helped to settle the Israelites' disagreements

5. **Who did the Israelites defeat with Deborah's help?** (Judges 4:24)

   a) the king of Canaan
   b) the king of Egypt
   c) the king of Assyria
   d) the king of Midian

6. **What did the angel of the Lord tell Gideon to do?** (Judges 6:14)

   a) tell the Israelites to turn away from their sin
   b) build the temple in Jerusalem
   c) save Israel from the Midianites
   d) lead the Israelites back to Egypt

7. **Why did Gideon think he wasn't good enough to do what the angel said?** (Judges 6:15)

   a) his family was weak and he was the least important family member
   b) he had leprosy and was too sick
   c) he wasn't good at public speaking
   d) he was poor

8. **How many men ended up fighting in Gideon's army?** (Judges 7:8)

   a) 100
   b) 300
   c) 10,000
   d) 22,000

Find the answers on page 178

Joshua became the new leader of the Israelites
after Moses died. He led them into the promised land.

Crossword Puzzle

ACROSS

3. God told Joshua to have twelve men pick up _____ from the river (Joshua 4:2–3)

6. The woman who was saved in Jericho because she helped the spies (Joshua 6:23)

8. The first time Gideon asked God for a sign, God put _____ on the wool but the ground was dry (Judges 6:37)

11. Gideon knew that the _____ was the real leader of Israel (Judges 8:23)

12. The Israelites _____ around the city of Jericho for seven days (Joshua 6:3–4)

DOWN

1. The first time God made Gideon's army smaller, he had ten _____ men who remained (Judges 7:3)

2. The number of times the Israelites marched around Jericho on each of the first six days (Joshua 6:3)

4. Before Joshua died, he said that he and his family would _____ the Lord (Joshua 24:15)

5. Deborah and a commander named Barak _____ to praise God after their victory (Judges 5:1)

7. Deborah was a _____ (Judges 4:4 NKJV)

9. The region where Deborah served as a judge (Judges 4:5)

10. Gideon broke down an _____ to a false god (Judges 6:28)

Find the answers on page 179

Word Search

Can you find all the words?
Words may be forward, backward, or up-and-down.

JOSHUA   ARMY   MIDIAN

TRUMPET   GIDEON   JORDAN

WALL   RIVER   JUDGE

CANAAN   JERICHO   DEBORAH

```
P T T R U M P E T H D E B B H O D D
J T R H K D E B O R A H N R D S G B
O J O H C I R E J H M W A L L D B A
S B V I Y C A N A A N K L H N R N R
H C N T R I V E R W F R N B K D G M
U X S R E G D U J B D G H R S W C Y
A B N D M I D I A N B R V R W A Q T
N M K T G I D E O N T N A D R O J W
```

Find the answers on page 179

Connect the Dots

Starting with number 1, draw a line to each number in order to create a picture.

Old Testament Heroes

Joshua, Esther, and Daniel were three brave people who loved and obeyed God. Their stories of bravery are found in the Old Testament.

WHAT DO YOU KNOW ABOUT JOSHUA, ESTHER, AND DANIEL?

1. **After Moses died, Joshua became the new leader of the Israelites. What did God tell Joshua to do?**
(Joshua 1:2)

   a) go back to Egypt
   b) climb a mountain
   c) lead the Israelites across the Jordan River
   d) go on a picnic

2. **Why did God want the people to go into Canaan?** (Exodus 6:8)

   a) to enter the land God promised to Abraham
   b) to meet their new neighbors
   c) to have better food
   d) to see more animals

3. **What did God tell the people to place on the side of the river after they finished crossing it?** (Joshua 4:1–3)

   a) their shoes
   b) their backpacks
   c) a pile of twelve stones
   d) a bucket of water from the river

4. **What place of honor did Esther receive?** (Esther 2:16–17)

   a) she became a princess
   b) she became a queen
   c) she became the president
   d) she was adopted by the king

5. **How did God use Esther?**
(Esther 8:3–6)

   a) she hid some spies
   b) she gave beauty treatments to her friends
   c) she saved the Jewish people from being killed
   d) she taught cooking lessons

6. **What king did Daniel work for?**
(Daniel 6:1–2)

   a) King Henry
   b) King David
   c) King Herod
   d) King Darius

7. **Why was Daniel thrown in the lions' den?** (Daniel 6:10–12)

   a) he prayed to God when it was against the king's law
   b) the den needed to be cleaned
   c) the lions were hungry
   d) the king was jealous of Daniel

8. **Why didn't the lions hurt Daniel?**
(Daniel 6:21–22)

   a) they were sleeping
   b) they didn't have any teeth
   c) they had just eaten a big meal
   d) God sent an angel to protect Daniel

Find the answers on page 179

Matching

Which hero's story matches each picture on the right?

JOSHUA

ESTHER

DANIEL

NOAH

MOSES

ELIJAH

WIDOW

Find the answers on page 179

Word Art

Color the letters and words for some of the books in the Old Testament: Major & Minor Prophets.

Daniel prayed and was protected while he was held captive in the den of _____.

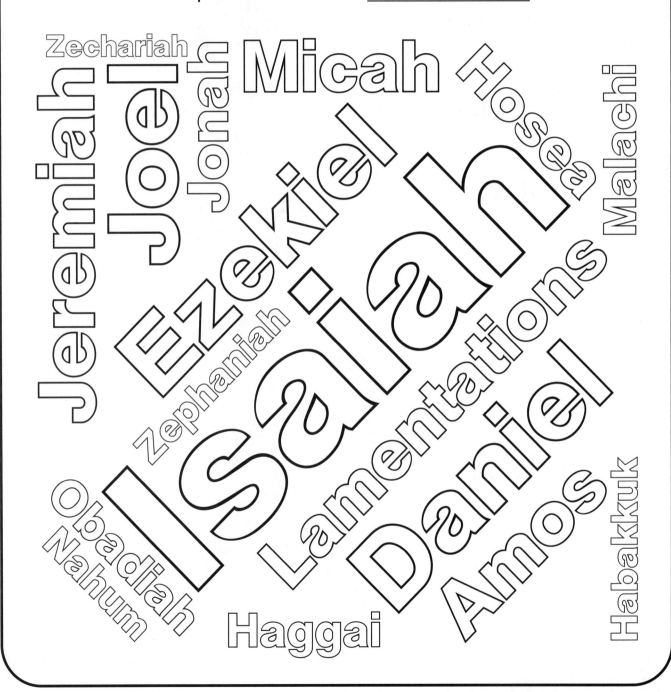

Find the answer on page 179

Crossword Puzzle

ACROSS

4. The number of months Esther had to do beauty treatments before she could meet King Xerxes (Esther 2:12)

5. God sent an _____ to help Elijah when he ran away to Horeb (1 Kings 19:5)

6. Mordecai treated Esther as his own _____ (Esther 2:7)

7. God used Elisha to raise a woman's _____ from the dead (2 Kings 4:36–37)

11. Esther told Mordecai she could only see the king if he held out his golden _____ (Esther 4:11)

DOWN

1. Elijah told a widow that God would do a miracle and give her enough _____ and oil until the rain came back (1 Kings 17:14)

2. What animals did God send to feed Elijah? (1 Kings 17:2–4)

3. The number of times Elisha told Naaman to wash in the river (2 Kings 5:10)

6. Elisha asked Elijah to give him a _____ share of his spirit (2 Kings 2:9)

8. Elisha did a miracle by helping a widow fill jars with this kind of oil (2 Kings 4:2)

9. The queen Esther replaced (Esther 1:19)

10. God sent _____ to Elijah's altar when he challenged the prophets of Baal (1 Kings 18:38)

Find the answers on page 180

Word Search

Can you find all the words?
Words may be forward, up-and-down, or diagonal.

ALTAR	ELISHA	OIL
ARMY	FIRE	OLIVE
DRY GROUND	JAR	PHARAOH
ELIJAH	MOSES	WIDOW

```
G B N D N M K P W S A R
H B C D W E L I S H A B D Q
D F O L I V E D W S Q O X M R N
Q F B M R T W S D H C X D Q S O G H
A B I W Q S X G H K L P M N R H G S W B
R M R W P H A R A O H R V N D N K S E B
M R E B Q L M D R Y G R O U N D R C M S
Y K N C S X Z W Q R W H N S D V J M B H
E L I J A H K D B X Q W H N K A W B
P T B L R W N M C S O Q K Q R M
K R T B N D M K Q B I Q M W
G A B M K B Z O X W L K
R G H Q D B D W Z B
D C W I D O W B
```

Find the answers on page 180

The First Kings of Israel

The Israelites wanted a king like the other nations had. God knew this was their way of rejecting Him as their Lord, but He gave the people what they wanted. Saul was the first king of Israel, followed by David and Solomon.

WHAT DO YOU KNOW ABOUT FIRST THREE KINGS OF ISRAEL?

1. How old was Saul when he became the king of Israel? (1 Samuel 13:1)

   a) 10
   b) 30
   c) 45
   d) 97

2. How did David help when King Saul was feeling sad? (1 Samuel 16:23 NKJV)

   a) he played his harp
   b) he gave the king a purple robe
   c) he made goat stew
   d) he played checkers with Saul

3. How did David fight the enemy giant Goliath? (1 Samuel 17:49)

   a) he used karate
   b) he used a slingshot and a stone
   c) he used a bow and arrow
   d) he used a club

4. Why was the kingdom of Israel taken away from Saul? (1 Samuel 13:13–14)

   a) he was lazy
   b) he was a bad soldier
   c) he didn't obey God's command
   d) he married a woman from another country

5. How many years did David rule as king? (2 Samuel 5:4)

   a) 10
   b) 20
   c) 30
   d) 40

6. David wrote over seventy psalms in the Bible—what does he call God in Psalm 23?

   a) my King
   b) my Ruler
   c) my Shepherd
   d) my Friend

7. What did Solomon ask God to give him when he became king? (2 Chronicles 1:10)

   a) gold and silver
   b) sheep and goats
   c) health and strength
   d) wisdom and knowledge

8. What did King Solomon get to do that his father, David, could not? (1 Chronicles 22:7–9)

   a) build the temple in Jerusalem
   b) train his army to fight the Philistines
   c) build houses for all the Israelites
   d) perform miracles

Find the answers on page 180

David was a shepherd who wrote many psalms.
Psalm 23:1 (NIrV) says, "The LORD is my shepherd.
He gives me everything I need."

Crossword Puzzle

ACROSS

2. The name of David's son who became king (1 Kings 2:12)
4. Who was Solomon's mother? (1 Kings 2:13)
5. In what book of the Bible can we find David's songs and prayers?
7. One of the weapons Goliath carried against David (1 Samuel 17:45)
8. Who was David's father? (1 Samuel 17:17)
10. Who anointed David's head with oil? (1 Samuel 16:13)
11. For how many years was Solomon the king of Israel? (1 Kings 11:42)

DOWN

1. Who was David's best friend? (1 Samuel 18:1)
3. Saul was _____ than other people (1 Samuel 9:2)
6. How many brothers did David have? (1 Samuel 16:10)
7. What David was before he became a king (1 Samuel 16:11)
9. The name of Jonathan's father (1 Samuel 14:1)

Find the answers on page 180

David said to Goliath . . . "This day the
_____ will give me the victory over you."

1 Samuel 17:45-46 NIrV

Find the Match

Draw a line from the crown on the left
to the matching crown on the right.

Find the answers on page 181

Unscramble the Words

Acts 13:22 has God's words about David.
Below, five words in this verse are scrambled.
Rewrite the verse with all the words written correctly.

"I have dofnu David son of sseje,

a man trefa my own rateh;

he will do itnyregveh

I want him to do."

_____

_____

_____

_____

Find the answers on page 181

David ruled over the whole nation of _____.
He did what was fair and right for all his people.

2 Samuel 8:15 NIrV

Word Art

Color the letters and words about the life of David.

When David was a boy, he fought and conquered
_____ with his sling and stone.

Find the answers on page 181

Be Wise

The Bible has many chapters and verses that show how God can help us make good decisions when we follow Him. Psalms and Proverbs are two of the "wisdom" books of the Bible.

WHAT DO YOU KNOW ABOUT PSALMS AND PROVERBS?

1. **What name is given to God in Psalm 23?**

   a) Friend
   b) Leader
   c) King
   d) Shepherd

2. **According to Psalm 33:12, what kind of nation does God bless?**

   a) a nation with a strong army
   b) a nation with rich people
   c) a nation whose God is the Lord
   d) a nation with cool flags

3. **According to Psalm 92:1, what is a good thing to do?**

   a) get good grades in school
   b) help your mom with the dishes
   c) praise God
   d) read good books

4. **What can help us when we are tempted to sin?** (Psalm 119:11)

   a) having good friends
   b) knowing God's word
   c) closing our eyes
   d) going for a walk

5. **What does Proverbs 3:5–6 tell us to do so that God will lead and direct our lives?**

   a) go to church on Sunday
   b) obey the 10 commandments
   c) be kind to your friends
   d) trust Him with all our heart

6. **How do we get wisdom and knowledge?** (Proverbs 9:10)

   a) by fearing and knowing God
   b) by reading the dictionary
   c) by getting enough sleep
   d) by watching TV

7. **According to Proverbs 17:22, what is good medicine?**

   a) a glass of milk
   b) fish oil
   c) a cheerful heart
   d) green tea

8. **What is better than having riches?** (Proverbs 22:1)

   a) having lots of friends
   b) having a good name (reputation)
   c) eating lots of vegetables
   d) winning a trophy

Find the answers on page 181

Word Search

Can you find all the words?
Words may be forward, backward, or up-and-down.

BIBLE	KNOWLEDGE	SHEPHERD
BLESS	LORD	TRUST
GOOD	PRAISE	UNDERSTANDING
HEART	PROVERBS	WISDOM

```
K M C Z Q R O N S R B S D B R H E A R T H K
R W H U N D E R S T A N D I N G K L N N T Y
D T C M O D S I W C T F T R U S T M L Y K N
E L B I B Q W P K Q P R A I S E W D O M Q D
K N O W L E D G E T R P S H E P H E R D G B
P D W Q G H S O E R T S P Q T S F W D H R W
W M D B Q P R O V E R B S F S T M Q R X C H
M B S B N T T D H G B L E S S W X C R N P
K L P W B R S C F W S D Q T Y D F X Z R M R
```

Find the answers on page 181

Crossword Puzzle

ACROSS

3. The Holy Spirit helps us to _____ God's Word (Job 32:8)
7. A person who takes care of sheep (Psalm 78:70–71)
8. Another word for "psalm" (Psalm 98:1)
10. Reading the Bible helps us to _____ (Psalm 19:7)
11. Solomon wrote many wise sayings in the book of _____

DOWN

1. A person who leads other people (Psalm 48:14)
2. Telling God how wonderful He is (Psalm 150)
4. Who wrote many of the Psalms? (Psalm 72:20)
5. God wants us to _____ Him (Proverbs 3:5)
6. There are 31 of these in the book of Proverbs
9. What word describes God in Psalm 48:1?
10. Another name for the Bible is God's _____

Find the answers on page 182

More Prophets

God's people started to love other things more than they loved Him. God sent prophets to warn the people that they needed to return to Him in love.

WHAT DO YOU KNOW ABOUT SOME OF GOD'S PROPHETS?

1. **Why is Jeremiah's nickname "the weeping prophet"?** (Jeremiah 9:1)

   a) he was happy to see the temple finished
   b) he was sad about what was going happen to the Israelites
   c) he had allergies and his eyes watered
   d) he was blind

2. **Why did Jeremiah think he wasn't good enough to be God's prophet?** (Jeremiah 1:6)

   a) he was young and didn't speak well
   b) he was poor
   c) the Israelites didn't like him
   d) he had no children to follow his footsteps

3. **Whose house did God use to give Jeremiah a message for the people?** (Jeremiah 18:1–2)

   a) a doctor's
   b) a teacher's
   c) a baker's
   d) a potter's

4. **What name did the Babylonians give to Daniel?** (Daniel 1:7)

   a) Shadrach
   b) Belteshazzar
   c) Meshach
   d) Abednego

5. **What promise did Daniel keep so that he wouldn't break God's rules?** (Daniel 1:8)

   a) he walked into town instead of riding a horse
   b) he melted all of his gold so it couldn't be turned into an idol
   c) he wouldn't take the king's food or wine
   d) he didn't speak so he wouldn't tell a lie

6. **Why was Daniel thrown into the lions' den?** (Daniel 6:10)

   a) he wouldn't bow down to the statue of the king
   b) his brothers were jealous that he had become an important helper to the king
   c) he prayed to God three times a day even though it was against the king's law
   d) his friend told a lie and said that Daniel had stolen the king's gold cup

7. **Which city did God tell Jonah to go to?** (Jonah 1:1–2)

   a) Bethlehem
   b) Tarshish
   c) Nazareth
   d) Nineveh

8. **How long was Jonah in the belly of a huge fish?** (Jonah 1:17)

   a) three days and three nights
   b) seven days
   c) twelve days and twelve nights
   d) forty days

Find the answers on page 182

Daniel prayed to God three times every day.
God protected Daniel in the lions' den.

Crossword Puzzle

ACROSS

4. What river did God's people have to cross? (Joshua 3:1)
5. God's people who wandered in the wilderness (Numbers 14:2)
6. Daniel prayed to God on his _____ (Daniel 6:10)
8. What king passed a law that the people had to pray only to him? (Daniel 6:7–9)
9. Who did Daniel only pray to? (Daniel 6:10)
10. The people Esther saved were _____ (Esther 8:3)

DOWN

1. Esther became a _____ (Esther 2:17)
2. God sent an _____ to protect Daniel (Daniel 6:22)
3. How many times a day did Daniel pray? (Daniel 6:10)
4. Who led the people after Moses died? (Joshua 1:1)
6. The person who rules a kingdom (Deuteronomy 17:15)
7. Daniel spent a night with these animals (Daniel 6:22)

Find the answers on page 182

God used Queen Esther to
save her people from an evil plan.

Crossword Puzzle

ACROSS

3. Who did God send to shut the lions' mouths so Daniel would be safe? (Daniel 6:22)

5. God said that Israel was like clay and He was like a _____ (Jeremiah 18:5–6)

7. Where did Jonah go when God told him to go to Nineveh? (Jonah 1:3)

11. God commanded the fish to spit Jonah out on dry _____ (Jonah 2:10)

12. God chose Jeremiah to be a _____ to the nations (Jeremiah 1:5)

DOWN

1. God helped Daniel read the writing on the _____ that no one else could understand (Daniel 5:5)

2. Where did the Israelites go when they didn't listen to the message God gave Jeremiah? (Jeremiah 43:6–7)

4. Whose dream did Daniel explain? (Daniel 2:28)

6. The place Daniel lived after the Israelites were defeated (Daniel 1:1)

8. What was wrapped around Jonah's head while he was in the belly of the fish? (Jonah 2:5)

9. God told Jeremiah to write the words He spoke on a _____ (Jeremiah 36:1–2)

10. The people of Nineveh _____ God's warning (Jonah 3:5)

Find the answers on page 182

Word Search

Can you find all the words?
Words may be forward, backward, or up-and-down.

JEREMIAH	POTTER	SCROLL
NINEVEH	WEEPING	LIONS
DANIEL	FISH	TARSHISH
JONAH	PRAY	MOUTH

```
D N L D A N I E L M N S
J H D W H S I F K W Q C
E N L N L I O N S B D R
R H N B R F Y C S H G O
E W R K R E T T O P J L
M K B S D P R A Y H O L
I S M O U T H B F V N L
A W E E P I N G W N A P
H V N I N E V E H N H V
T R H S T A R S H I S H
```

Find the answers on page 183

The First Christmas

Jesus came from His beautiful home in heaven to a humble place on earth. But God had a plan and purpose for sending His Son to earth. Jesus was the promised Messiah. He would forgive people of their sins and make them right with God.

WHAT DO YOU KNOW ABOUT WHEN JESUS WAS BORN?

1. **Where was Jesus born?** (Luke 2:4–6)

   a) Nazareth
   b) Bethlehem
   c) Galilee
   d) Jerusalem

2. **Who were Jesus's parents on earth?** (Luke 1:27)

   a) Zechariah and Elizabeth
   b) Abraham and Sarah
   c) Jacob and Rachel
   d) Joseph and Mary

3. **How did Jesus's parents find out they were going to have a baby?** (Luke 1:28)

   a) the king told them
   b) an angel shared the news
   c) they got a letter in the mail
   d) baby Jesus was dropped off on their doorstep

4. **Who did the angel first tell about Jesus's birth?** (Luke 2:8–11)

   a) shepherds
   b) King Herod
   c) wise men
   d) John the Baptist

5. **What appeared in the sky when Jesus was born?** (Matthew 2:1–2)

   a) fireworks
   b) lightning
   c) a bright star
   d) the Goodyear blimp

6. **Which of the following was not a gift the wise men brought to Jesus?** (Matthew 2:11)

   a) gold
   b) silver
   c) frankincense
   d) myrrh

7. **Where did baby Jesus sleep the night He was born?** (Luke 2:6–7)

   a) in a crib
   b) on a throne
   c) in a basket
   d) in a manger

8. **Who told the wise men he wanted to find baby Jesus?** (Matthew 2:7-8)

   a) King Xerxes
   b) King Herod
   c) King David
   d) King Darius

Find the answers on page 183

Crossword Puzzle

ACROSS

2. The angel who told Mary that she would have a baby (see Luke 1:26)
5. Where did Mary and Joseph go to register for the census? (Luke 2:4)
7. What did the wise men follow to find Jesus? (Matthew 2:9)
8. Joseph was a relative of King _____ (see Luke 2:4)
10. Jesus's relative, who was born shortly before Him (see Luke 1:57–60)
11. Mary wrapped Jesus in strips of _____ (Luke 2:12)

DOWN

1. Mary kept all these things like a treasure in her _____ (Luke 2:19)
3. An _____ told the shepherds that Jesus was born (Luke 2:8–9)
4. The king who wanted to hurt Jesus shortly after He was born (Matthew 2:16)
6. The wise men came from the _____ looking for baby Jesus (Matthew 2:1)
7. Jesus came to be our _____ (Luke 2:11)
9. There was no room for Mary and Joseph to stay at this place (Luke 2:7)

Find the answers on page 183

Finish the Picture

Complete the scene of the first Christmas below by drawing the stable, the star, and some of the visitors who came to meet baby Jesus (shepherds, animals, angels).

Word Search

Can you find all the words?
Words may be forward, backward, or up-and-down.

ANGELS   JESUS   SAVIOR

BETHLEHEM   JOSEPH   SHEPHERDS

HEROD   MANGER   STAR

INN   MARY   WISE MEN

```
R I M H M A R Y L P F V J E S U S B S G
T N C B E T H L E H E M S D B N S T T R
N D G Q S X Z S H E P H E R D S G A
B W I S E M E N N K E L B K T S D R
S D O R E H K N G J O S E P H S M M
N R O I V A S M E S S L E G N A
H E R D S R M A N G E R H O
```

Crossword Puzzle

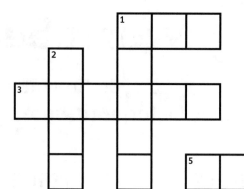

ACROSS

1. The angel told Mary her baby would be called the Son of _____ (Luke 1:35)

3. The name of Jesus's earthly father (Luke 2:22)

5. An angel spoke to Joseph in a _____ (Matthew 1:20)

6. Who were the first people to visit baby Jesus? (Luke 2:15–17)

10. The name of the angel who visited Mary (Luke 1:26–27)

11. What was the name of the man who baptized Jesus? (Matthew 3:13)

DOWN

1. The angel told Mary that Jesus would be _____ (Luke 1:32)

2. What insects did John the Baptist eat? (Matthew 3:4)

4. Bethlehem was also called the town of _____ (Luke 2:4)

7. The name of Mary's relative who was also going to have a baby (Luke 1:36)

8. Who told Simeon he would see the Messiah before he died? (Luke 2:26)

9. The town where Mary lived (Luke 1:26–27)

Find the answers on page 184

Make as many words as you can out of the letters in
Bethlehem

_____   _____

_____   _____

_____   _____

_____   _____

_____   _____

_____   _____

_____   _____

_____   _____

_____   _____

Maze

Help the shepherd get to the manger.

Find the answers on page 184

Word Search

Can you find all the words?
Words may be forward, backward, or up-and-down.

JESUS JOHN ELIZABETH

ANNA MESSIAH SIMEON

ANGEL JOSEPH GABRIEL

MARY SHEEP SHEPHERDS

```
K D S H E P H E R D S H M H B J
M H P P G K M P E E H S K R L O
A B R L T G A B R I E L M Q G H
R K N H S U S J E S U S W Q D N
Y N B C D L R J T A N N A K L B
K N G L L E G N A V J L N P H R
S M S I M E O N K M J O S E P H
H T E B A Z I L E K Z D Z L W B
M S H S M E S S I A H K L T N D
```

Find the answers on page 184

Searching for Jesus

When Jesus was born, a bright star appeared in the sky. Some wise men who studied the stars knew this was a sign that the Messiah had been born. They set out on a long journey to find Jesus by following the star.

WHAT DO YOU KNOW ABOUT THE VISIT OF THE WISE MEN?

1. **From which direction did the wise men travel?** (Matthew 2:1)

   a) north
   b) south
   c) east
   d) west

2. **What reason did the wise men give for coming to Jerusalem?** (Matthew 2:2)

   a) they came to visit the temple
   b) they wanted to meet King Herod
   c) they came to worship the newborn king
   d) they wanted ride their camels

3. **Where could the wise men find the newborn Messiah?** (Matthew 2:4–5)

   a) Galilee
   b) Nazareth
   c) Canaan
   d) Bethlehem

4. **What did King Herod tell the wise men to do?** (Matthew 2:8)

   a) report back to him after they found the child
   b) spread the good news about Jesus's birth
   c) bring food and water along
   d) write down everything that happened

5. **How did the wise men find Jesus?** (Matthew 2:9)

   a) soldiers led the way
   b) an angel guided them
   c) their camels knew where to go
   d) the star stopped over the place where Jesus was

6. **What did the wise men do when they found Jesus with Mary?** (Matthew 2:11)

   a) they ate dinner with them
   b) they washed their feet
   c) they bowed down and worshiped Jesus
   d) they gave their camels a drink

7. **What gifts did the wise men give to Jesus?** (Matthew 2:11)

   a) gold, silver, and myrrh
   b) gold, frankincense, and myrrh
   c) gold, silver, and bronze
   d) olive oil, grapes, and bread

8. **Why didn't the wise men go back to see Herod?** (Matthew 2:12)

   a) they were too tired
   b) they wanted to go home
   c) they were warned in a dream
   d) they didn't have gifts for him

Find the answers on page 184

Finish the Picture

Complete the scene of the wise men traveling to
Bethlehem by drawing the wise men riding their camels,
buildings in the background, and stars in the sky.

The wise men brought special gifts for Jesus—
gold, frankincense, and myrrh.

Word Search

Can you find all the words?
Words may be forward, backward, or up-and-down.

CAMELS   KING   REPORT

EAST   GOLD   TRAVEL

ANGEL   MYRRH   DREAM

STAR   HEROD   JESUS

```
G H M D R E A M D R J E S U S
M Y H N R R H E R O D N K F T
Y S M T R A V E L C M B T H A
R B D S L E M A C M N T L S R
R E P O R T S W N L E G N A M
H R G H E A S T D H N B R S D
K L M K I N G N D G L N K L N
T V L R B M G O L D M N K B S
```

Find the answers on page 185

Crossword Puzzle

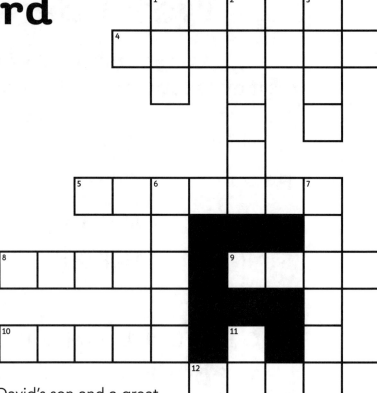

ACROSS

4. This relative of Jesus was David's son and a great king of Israel (Matthew 1:6)
5. The distant relative of Jesus who was the father of many nations (Genesis 17:4–5)
8. The tribe of Israel that Jesus came from (Revelation 5:5)
9. The relative of Jesus who was King David's great-grandmother (Matthew 1:5)
10. In the family line of Jesus listed in the book of Matthew, what name is shared by two different people? (Matthew 1:2, 16)
12. Abraham's son who fulfilled God's promise to create a great family (Genesis 17:19)

DOWN

1. The family line of Jesus in the book of Luke goes all the way back to ___ (Luke 3:38)
2. The name of Jesus's earthly father (Matthew 1:16)
3. This relative of Jesus built a large boat to survive a flood (Luke 3:36)
6. This woman became part of Jesus's family line after she hid two Israelite spies in Jericho (Joshua 2:3–4)
7. Who was Jesus's earthly great-grandfather? (Luke 3:23–24)
11. Jacob was in Jesus's family line instead of his older twin brother, ____ (Genesis 25:23–26)

Find the answers on page 185

Jesus's Early Life

Mary and Joseph took Jesus to the temple when He was a baby. It was part of a special rule God had given to His people. When Jesus grew up, He was baptized before He started His work of telling people about God's kingdom.

WHAT DO YOU KNOW ABOUT JESUS'S BAPTISM?

1. **What was the name of the man who was at the temple when Mary and Joseph brought Jesus?** (Luke 2:25–28)

   a) Simeon
   b) Eli
   c) Samuel
   d) Aaron

2. **What had the Holy Spirit told the man who was at the temple?** (Luke 2:26)

   a) He would be taken to heaven in a chariot of fire
   b) He would meet John the Baptist
   c) He would see the Messiah
   d) He would rebuild the temple

3. **When the man who was at the temple held Jesus, what did he say to God?** (Luke 2:30)

   a) "Thank You!"
   b) "You are good!"
   c) "Blessed be Your Name!"
   d) "I have seen your salvation."

4. **Who else met Jesus at the temple?** (Luke 2:36)

   a) Elizabeth
   b) Anna
   c) Joanna
   d) Martha

5. **When Jesus grew up, who baptized Him?** (Matthew 3:13)

   a) Paul
   b) John the Baptist
   c) Peter
   d) James the Disciple

6. **As Jesus was being baptized, the Holy Spirit came down in the form of a _____** (Luke 3:22)

   a) dove
   b) flame
   c) tree
   d) crown

7. **What did God say from heaven when Jesus was baptized?** (Luke 3:22)

   a) "This is my Son. Listen to Him!"
   b) "Jesus will save the world."
   c) "Go find Your disciples."
   d) "You are my Son and I love you. I am very pleased with you."

8. **When Jesus began preaching God's Good News, what did He say?** (Mark 1:15)

   a) "The kingdom of God is near."
   b) "Prepare the way!"
   c) "I am God's Son."
   d) "Come, follow me."

Find the answers on page 185

When Jesus was a boy,
He went to the temple.
Everyone was amazed
by His wisdom.

Word Art

Color the letters and words about the life of Jesus.

The story of the birth of Jesus can be found in the New Testament of the Bible. The two books that describe His birth are _____ and _____.

Find the answers on page 185

Isaiah Tells Us About Jesus

Isaiah was a prophet who wrote the Old Testament book of Isaiah. He received messages and visions from God concerning God's people. He warned the Israelites that they would be punished if they turned away from God, but he also reminded them of God's love and the promise of a Messiah.

WHAT DO YOU KNOW ABOUT ISAIAH'S MESSAGES OF JESUS?

1. **What is one of the names that Jesus would be called?** (Isaiah 7:14)
   a) Joseph
   b) John
   c) Immanuel
   d) Isaiah

2. **What did Isaiah say would happen shortly before Jesus began His earthly ministry?** (Isaiah 40:3)
   a) ten angels would appear in the sky
   b) a messenger would announce His coming
   c) kings would look for Him
   d) it would rain for 40 days

3. **What would God's Spirit give to Jesus?** (Isaiah 11:2)
   a) joy and peace
   b) health and happiness
   c) gold and silver
   d) wisdom and understanding

4. **What is something great that would happen to Jesus?** (Isaiah 52:13)
   a) He would be highly honored and exalted
   b) He would become the prince of Egypt
   c) He would become the governor of Rome
   d) He would be given a gold chariot

5. **What did Isaiah say that Jesus would do for us?** (Isaiah 53:5)
   a) He would stay on earth for 70 years
   b) He would tame wild animals
   c) He would protect us from bad rulers
   d) He would take the punishment for our sins

6. **Isaiah foretold what Jesus would do while He was treated harshly before His accusers. Which of the following is correct?** (Isaiah 53:7)
   a) He would run away from His accusers.
   b) He would be silent
   c) He would call for help
   d) He would laugh at them

7. **What is another reason Jesus came?** (Isaiah 61:1)
   a) to get rid of sickness and disease
   b) to teach people how to fish
   c) to make everyone rich
   d) to comfort the brokenhearted

8. **What does Isaiah tell us about Jesus in Isaiah 53:9?**
   a) He never teased His brothers
   b) He never talked back to His mother
   c) He never lied or hurt anyone
   d) He never cried

Find the answers on page 185

Word Search

Can you find all the words?
Words may be forward or backward.

MESSIAH   SIMEON   ANNA   TEMPLE

BAPTIZE   JOHN   JORDAN   DOVE

WATER   PRIEST   PREPARE   VOICE

```
      V O I C E N G
    J O R D A N B S R T H
  P R H M P R E P A R E K R H P
  K M S S H A I S S E M N G R S
  N H D O V E S R H N H O J N T
  P S M P R I E S T N N A N N A
  H E Z I T P A B N W A T E R W
  M S S I M E O N K H M
      T E M P L E G
```

Find the answers on page 186

Connect the Dots

Starting with number 1, keep drawing a line
to the next number to create a picture.

The Twelve Disciples

Jesus chose twelve men to be His helpers. The "disciples" were ordinary men who followed Jesus during His years of teaching and doing miracles. They did not understand everything He taught them, but they were faithful to help Him while He lived on earth.

WHAT DO YOU KNOW ABOUT JESUS'S TWELVE DISCIPLES?

1. **What did Jesus say to Simon Peter and his brother Andrew?** (Matthew 4:18–19)

   a) "It's a beautiful morning!"
   b) "Did you catch any fish?"
   c) "Where is your boat?"
   d) "Come, follow me."

2. **What were the names of two other brothers that Jesus called to follow Him?** (Matthew 4:21)

   a) James and Matthew
   b) John and George
   c) James and John
   d) Peter and Paul

3. **Who was not among Jesus's original twelve disciples?** (Luke 6:13–16)

   a) Simon Peter
   b) Philip
   c) Bartholomew
   d) Paul

4. **What did Jesus tell the disciples when parents brought their children to Him?** (Matthew 19:14)

   a) "Send the children away."
   b) "Give them something to eat."
   c) "Let the children come to me."
   d) "It's time for them to sleep."

5. **What did Philip ask Jesus to do?** (John 14:8)

   a) turn water into wine
   b) show the disciples the Father
   c) heal his mother
   d) make it rain

6. **What did Peter do that none of the other disciples did?** (Matthew 14:29)

   a) turn stones into bread
   b) heal ten lepers
   c) call Jesus his friend
   d) walk on the water

7. **What did Peter tell Jesus in Matthew 16:15–16?**

   a) "You are the Messiah, the Son of the living God."
   b) "You are my brother and friend."
   c) "You are my leader and teacher."
   d) "You are healer and Savior."

8. **What bad thing did Judas agree to do?** (Luke 22:3–6)

   a) break into the temple
   b) steal food from the poor
   c) turn Jesus over to His enemies
   d) give money to Jesus's enemies

Find the answers on page 186

Fill in the Blanks

Fill in the missing letters to list
the names of Jesus's Twelve Disciples.
(Turn to Luke 6:13-16 if you need help.)

S _ M O _   P E _ _ R

A N _ _ E _

J _ M _ _

J _ H _

P _ I _ I _

B A _ T H _ L _ M _ W

M _ T _ H _ _

T _ O _ A _

J A _ _ S
(son of Alphaeus)

S I _ _ N
(called the Zealot)

J _ D _ S
(son of James)

J U _ _ S   I S _ _ R _ _ T

Find the answers on page 186

"Come and _____ me," Jesus said.
"I will send you out to _____ for people."

(Matthew 4:19 NIrV)

Find the Message

Cross out the letters: B C V X and Z to read what Jesus told His disciples, then write it on the lines below:

Z I B X C W I B L L V X M C A K E Z B C Y O V U B

F X I S Z H E R S Z X O B F B C V B M X E V N X Z

_____

_____

_____

_____

_____

Find the answers on page 186

Crossword Puzzle

ACROSS

6. The name of Peter's brother (Matthew 4:18)
7. What was another name of Judas, who betrayed Jesus? (Mark 3:19)
8. How many disciples did Jesus select to follow Him? (Matthew 10:1)
9. When Jesus called the first disciples, what were they casting into the sea? (Matthew 4:20)
10. James's brother, who was also a disciple (Matthew 4:21)
11. Peter said _____ times that he didn't know Jesus (Mark 14:30)

DOWN

1. Levi was also called _____ (see Matthew 9:9 and Luke 5:27)
2. Thomas said he had to see the marks of the _____ in Jesus's hands (John 20:25)
3. Peter walked on the _____ toward Jesus (Matthew 14:29)
4. John and _____ saw the empty tomb after Jesus rose from the dead (John 20:3)
5. Who replaced Judas after he betrayed Jesus? (Acts 1:24–26)
8. Jesus gave James and John the nickname "sons of _____" (Mark 3:17)

Find the answers on page 187

Coded Message

Use the key below to match the symbols and fill in the missing words.

✿	◉	♣	❄	✳	◆	✳	★	❀	✪	✳	●	○
A	B	C	D	E	F	G	H	I	J	K	L	M

■	❑	▢	✳	❄	▲	▼	◆	❖	◗	✳	▮	✳
N	O	P	Q	R	S	T	U	V	W	X	Y	Z

HE ___ ___ ___ ___ ___ THE
★ ❄ ✿ ● ▲

___ ___ ___ ___ ___ ___ ___ ___ ___ ___ ___ ___ ___

AND ___ ___ ___ ___ ___ UP THEIR

___ ___ ___ ___ ___ ___ .
◗ ❑ ◆ ■ ❄ ▲

(Psalm 147:3)

Find the answers on page 187

Jesus Performs Miracles

Jesus did miracles for all kinds of people. He helped rich people and poor people. He used both young and old people to show God's glory through His miracles. He didn't look at the things most people see from the outside. Jesus cared about people's hearts.

WHAT DO YOU KNOW ABOUT THE PEOPLE IN JESUS'S MIRACLES?

1. Who did Jairus ask Jesus to heal? (Luke 8:42)

a) his daughter
b) his son
c) his mother
d) his wife

2. What was Jairus's job? (Luke 8:41)

a) tax collector
b) lawyer
c) doctor
d) ruler of a synagogue

3. What did Jesus tell Jairus to do for his request to be answered? (Luke 8:50)

a) offer a sacrifice at the temple
b) believe, and not be afraid
c) pray loudly in the city square
d) memorize the 23rd Psalm

4. Why was Jesus delayed in reaching Jairus's house? (Luke 8:42–48)

a) He raised Lazarus from the dead
b) He changed water into wine at a wedding
c) He healed a woman with a bleeding problem
d) He caught a fish with a coin in its mouth

5. Where was Jesus teaching when a hungry crowd of more than 5,000 surrounded him? (John 6:1)

a) by the Jordan River
b) by the Red Sea
c) by the Sea of Galilee
d) by the Jabbok River

6. Which disciple told Jesus about a boy with some food? (John 6:8–9)

a) Philip
b) Andrew
c) Peter
d) James

7. What exactly did the boy have? (John 6:9)

a) five fish and two loaves
b) a fish and two loaves
c) two fish and five loaves
d) seven fish and seven loaves

8. How many baskets were left over after Jesus miraculously fed the whole crowd? (John 6:13)

a) three
b) seven
c) ten
d) twelve

Find the answers on page 187

Jesus went all over Galilee. . . .
He _____ every illness and
sickness the people had.

Matthew 4:23 NIrV

Find the Match

Draw a line between the stone jars that are exactly alike.

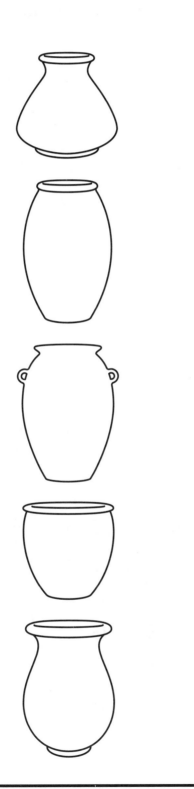

Find the answers on page 187

Word Search

Can you find all the words?
Words may be forward, backward, or diagonal.

WEDDING	STORM	LAZARUS
CANA	TOMB	BREAD
PEOPLE	FISH	CALM
WATER	WAVES	JARS

```
L K N D J A R S T R
C M L A C H K V J S R S
H S I F W V S N T O M B T H
N J D N G W N N X W A V E S
M R O T S C A H T B R K T L
Q N N A C R J T D B R E A D
K P S P E O P L E K H G B N
Z L A Z A R U S L R R T H M
V G N I D D E W L S V G
H G B A N A C Y S T
```

Find the answers on page 188

Crossword Puzzle

ACROSS

4. When Jesus went to Jairus's house, only Peter, _____, and John were allowed to go inside with Him (Luke 8:51)

5. The age of Jairus's daughter (Luke 8:42)

7. Which festival were the Jews celebrating when Jesus fed the big crowd? (John 6:4)

9. A woman who came to Jesus was _____ (Luke 8:47)

10. The crowd of 5,000 followed Jesus because they saw Him heal ____ people (John 6:2)

DOWN

1. Jesus asked _____ where they would get enough food to feed the people (John 6:5)

2. When Jairus came to Jesus, he fell down at Jesus's ____ (Luke 8:41)

3. When the disciples picked up the leftovers, they filled twelve _____ (John 6:13)

5. While Jairus was talking to Jesus, a woman came and _____ Jesus's clothes (Luke 8:44)

6. What did Jesus do to the bread after He looked up to heaven? (Luke 9:16)

8. When Jesus healed Jairus's daughter, He told the other people to give her something to _____ (Luke 8:55)

11. After Jesus fed the people, they wanted Him to be their ____ (John 6:15)

Find the answers on page 188

Maze

Follow the maze to help
the sick woman in the crowd get to Jesus.

Find the answers on page 188

Decode the Message

Using the key, decode the message below.

___ ___ ___ ___ ___   ___ ___   ___ ___ ___   ___ ___ ___ ___ ___
2 3 9 24 9   17 9   20 1 3   26 25 3 4 20

___ ___ ___ ___ ___ ___ .
1 3 4 22 3 25

KEY	
1 = H	14 = Y
2 = J	15 = X
3 = E	16 = D
4 = A	17 = I
5 = M	18 = K
6 = B	19 = N
7 = P	20 = T
8 = F	21 = V
9 = S	22 = L
10 = Z	23 = C
11 = O	24 = U
12 = Q	25 = R
13 = W	26 = G

Find the answers on page 188

Crossword Puzzle

ACROSS

2. Bartimaeus threw off his_____ when Jesus called him (Mark 10:50 NIrV)

4. Where did Jesus look to before He healed the deaf man? (Mark 7:34)

6. As soon as Bartimaeus was healed, he _____ Jesus on the road (Mark 10:52)

9. What did Jesus do before He touched the deaf man's tongue? (Mark 7:33)

11. The people who brought the deaf man to Jesus wanted Jesus to lay His _____ on the man (Mark 7:32)

12. Bartimaeus earned money by being a _____ (Mark 10:46)

DOWN

1. What was Bartimaeus sitting by when Jesus passed his way? (Mark 10:46)

3. Where had Jesus come back from when he healed the deaf man? (Mark 7:31)

5. When people saw Jesus heal the deaf man, they said Jesus does _____ well (Mark 7:37)

7. Bartimaeus called Jesus the Son of _____ (Mark 10:47)

8. The deaf man began to _____ clearly as soon as Jesus healed him (Mark 7:35)

10. The name of Bartimaeus's father (Mark 10:46)

Find the answers on page 189

Jesus's Stories

Jesus often told stories that had a special meaning. Those stories are called parables. Sometimes people were confused by His stories, but Jesus helped His followers understand the parables.

WHAT DO YOU KNOW ABOUT JESUS'S PARABLES?

1. **Who was a "neighbor" to a Jewish man who was hurt by robbers?** (Luke 10:30–37)

   a) a Levite
   b) a priest
   c) a Samaritan
   d) an innkeeper

2. **Which of these was not "lost" in the three parables Jesus told in Luke 15?**

   a) a wagon
   b) a sheep
   c) a coin
   d) a man's son

3. **What does Jesus teach in the parable of the Pharisee and the tax collector?** (Luke 18:10–14)

   a) we need to pray out loud
   b) we need to be humble
   c) we need to be proud
   d) we need to be kind

4. **In the parable of the sower, what do the seeds stand for?** (Mark 4:3–20)

   a) wheat
   b) corn
   c) the word of God
   d) fertilizer

5. **How is a mustard seed like the Kingdom of God?** (Mark 4:30–33)

   a) it feeds a lot of people
   b) everyone likes mustard
   c) it grows quickly
   d) it's a tiny seed but grows into a large plant

6. **In His parable of the lamp, what does Jesus say we should do?** (Matthew 5:14–16)

   a) let our light shine for Jesus
   b) sing songs of praise
   c) invite our neighbors to church
   d) read good books

7. **What did the wise man do before a big storm in one of Jesus's parables?** (Matthew 7:24–27)

   a) he built a boat
   b) he built his house on sandy ground
   c) he built his house on a rock
   d) he built a tower

8. **When do the angels in heaven rejoice?** (Luke 15:8–10)

   a) when we read the Bible
   b) when people get married
   c) when we go to church
   d) when someone becomes a Christian

Find the answers on page 189

Crossword Puzzle

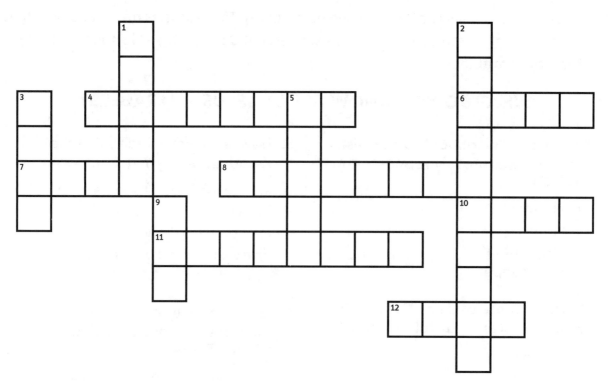

ACROSS

4. Many people _____ Jesus (Matthew 4:25)
6. The wise man built his house on this (Matthew 7:24)
7. Being a good neighbor means being _____ to others
8. Another name for the stories Jesus told (Matthew 13:34)
10. The size of a mustard seed (goes with "teeny"; see Mark 4:31)
11. The Samaritan was a good _____ (Luke 10:36–37)
12. What the foolish man built his house on (Matthew 7:26)

DOWN

1. The opposite of humble
2. People who believe in Jesus as their Savior
3. One of the books of the Bible where Jesus's parables are found
5. Jesus taught people while He lived on _____
9. In Luke 15:4–6, how many sheep were lost?

Find the answers on page 189

Coded Message

Use the key below to match the symbols of Jesus's message to letters to break the code!

Jesus traveled from town to town teaching people.
He told them to love God and love each other.

Crossword Puzzle

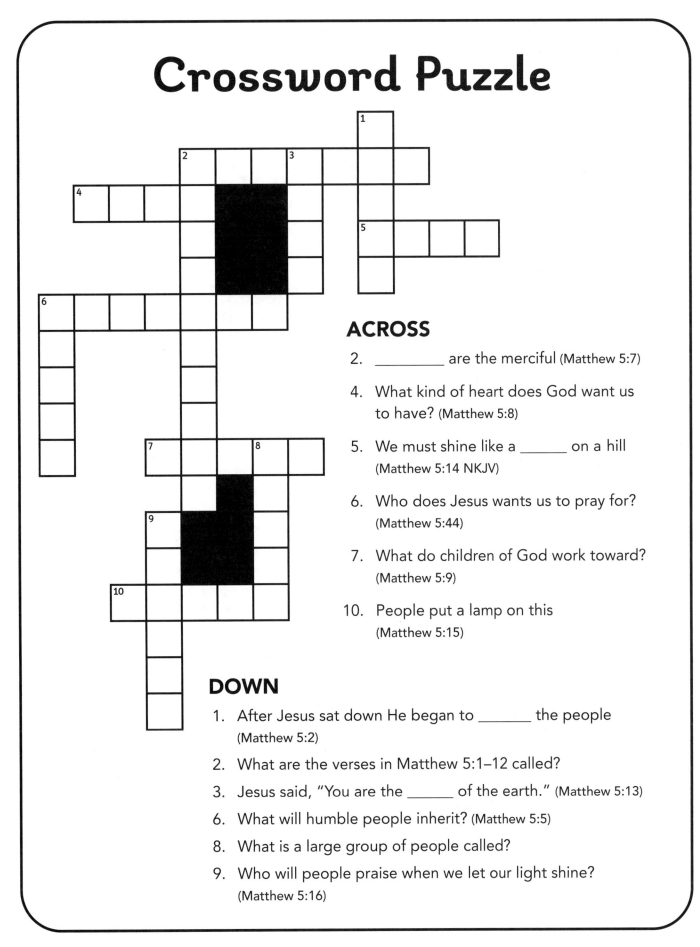

ACROSS

2. _____ are the merciful (Matthew 5:7)

4. What kind of heart does God want us to have? (Matthew 5:8)

5. We must shine like a _____ on a hill (Matthew 5:14 NKJV)

6. Who does Jesus wants us to pray for? (Matthew 5:44)

7. What do children of God work toward? (Matthew 5:9)

10. People put a lamp on this (Matthew 5:15)

DOWN

1. After Jesus sat down He began to _____ the people (Matthew 5:2)

2. What are the verses in Matthew 5:1–12 called?

3. Jesus said, "You are the _____ of the earth." (Matthew 5:13)

6. What will humble people inherit? (Matthew 5:5)

8. What is a large group of people called?

9. Who will people praise when we let our light shine? (Matthew 5:16)

Find the answers on page 190

Jesus's Special Friends

Jesus traveled though many towns and villages to heal people, bless little children, and tell people about God. But some of the people Jesus met became His special friends—like Mary and Martha and their brother Lazarus.

WHAT DO YOU KNOW ABOUT MARY, MARTHA, AND LAZARUS?

1. **What did Mary do when Jesus came to their home?** (Luke 10:38–39)

   a) she made coffee for Jesus
   b) she served Him breakfast
   c) she sat by Jesus and listened to Him
   d) she told Jesus stories

2. **What did Martha do while Jesus was at their house?** (Luke 10:40)

   a) she sang songs
   b) she was busy working in the house
   c) she played the tambourine
   d) she went outside to pick flowers

3. **Where did Mary, Martha, and Lazarus live?** (John 11:1)

   a) Bethany
   b) Nazareth
   c) Jerusalem
   d) Samaria

4. **What message did Mary and Martha send to Jesus?** (John 11:3)

   a) "It's time for dinner"
   b) "Help us find Lazarus"
   c) "We made a robe for you"
   d) "Your friend Lazarus is sick"

5. **What happened before Jesus came to their house?** (John 11:17)

   a) Lazarus got better
   b) Lazarus got leprosy
   c) Lazarus died
   d) Lazarus went to the hospital

6. **What miracle did Jesus do so the people would believe He was God's Son?** (John 11:41–44)

   a) He rolled the stone away from the tomb
   b) He raised Lazarus from the dead
   c) He made it lightning and thunder
   d) He caused an earthquake

7. **What did Martha do when Jesus came to their house for dinner again?** (John 12:2)

   a) she baked a fig cake for Jesus
   b) she made some grape juice
   c) she served the food
   d) she gave a speech

8. **What did Mary do?** (John 12:3)

   a) she helped Martha bake bread
   b) she poured the juice
   c) she washed the dishes
   d) she poured expensive perfume over Jesus's feet

Find the answers on page 190

Maze

Help Mary and Martha find their way
to their good friend Jesus!

Find the answers on page 190

Crossword Puzzle

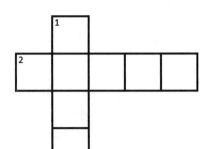

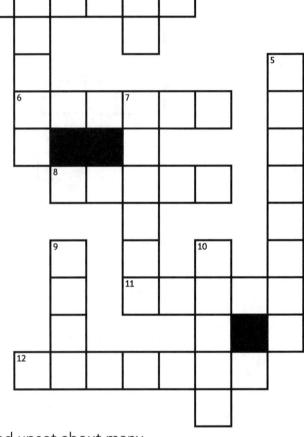

ACROSS

2. Martha let Jesus stay at her _____ (Luke 10:38)

4. What Jesus did before He called out to Lazarus (John 11:41–42)

6. Who was Mary's sister? (John 11:1)

8. Jesus said that Lazarus's sickness was for God's _____ (John 11:4)

11. What covered the entrance to the tomb where Lazarus was buried? (John 11:38–39)

12. When Lazarus came out of the tomb his body was _____ in strips of cloth (John 11:44)

DOWN

1. Jesus told Martha she was _____ and upset about many things (Luke 10:41)

3. What did Mary pour on Jesus's feet? (John 12:3)

5. Many of Mary's friends who saw what Jesus did _____ in Him (John 11:45)

7. Which disciple wanted to go with Jesus to see Lazarus? (John 11:16)

9. How many days was Lazarus dead before Jesus arrived? (John 11:17)

10. Jesus _____ Mary, Martha, and Lazarus (John 11:5)

Find the answers on page 190

Children followed Jesus too.
"Let the children come to me!" He said.

Make as many words as you can out of the letters in
Mountainside

Maze

Help take the little boy's lunch to Jesus!

Find the answers on page 191

Word Search

Can you find all the words?
Words may be forward or backward.

MOUNTAIN   HUMBLE   LAMP

MERCY   PEACE   EARTH

SALT   CITY   LIGHT

TEACH   BLESSED   COMFORT

```
              T L A S E
            M E R C Y C H
          B D E S S E L B T
        M F C O M F O R T G D
      C E A R T H D Y T I C A E
    N B M O U N T A I N T H F C M
  L I G H T N B P P E A C E P E J B
Q M H C A E T N B P L A M P E B A O H
N H B L H U M B L E T B L S S Z N T I J L
```

Find the answers on page 191

One stormy night, Jesus told the wind and waves
to be still, and just like that, the sea was calm.
His miracles showed people that He was God's Son.

Connect the Dots

Connect the dots below to see a message.

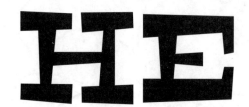

THE DEAF

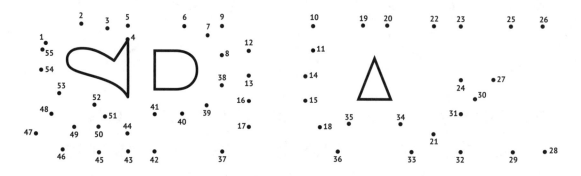

Teach Us to Pray

Prayer is talking to God. We can pray to thank God. We can pray when we're sad or scared, or to ask for things we need. Prayer can be powerful. Sometimes when we pray, God will do things that seem impossible. Jesus taught His disciples how to pray.

WHAT DO YOU KNOW ABOUT THE LORD'S PRAYER?

1. **When Jesus began His prayer, He called God our Father in _____.** (Matthew 6:9)
   a) heaven
   b) the sky
   c) outer space
   d) the temple

2. **How are we supposed to treat God's name?** (see Matthew 6:9)
   a) we should never say it out loud
   b) we should only call God "Lord"
   c) we should honor His name as holy
   d) we should say it however we want

3. **How much food or bread should we pray for each day?** (Matthew 6:11)
   a) enough for the whole year
   b) enough for our whole lives
   c) enough for one week
   d) enough for the day

4. **We should pray for God's _____ to come.** (Matthew 6:10)
   a) punishment
   b) kingdom
   c) angels
   d) help

5. **When we disobey God, what should we ask Him to do?** (Matthew 6:12)
   a) punish us
   b) forgive our sins
   c) look the other way
   d) bless us

6. **Who are we supposed to forgive?** (Matthew 6:12)
   a) people who apologize to us
   b) only people who are our friends
   c) other Christians
   d) anyone who does wrong to us

7. **What should we ask God to keep us from?** (Matthew 6:13)
   a) mean people
   b) danger
   c) temptation
   d) getting hurt

8. **Whose "will"—or whose plans and desires—should we pray for?** (see Matthew 6:10)
   a) God's
   b) our own
   c) our parents'
   d) our teachers'

Find the answers on page 191

Fill in the Blanks

Try to fill in as many blanks as you can
without looking at your Bible!

Our _____ in heaven,

Hallowed be Your _____.

Your _____ come.

Your _____ be done

On _____ as it is in _____.

Give us this day our daily _____.

And _____ us our debts,

As we _____ our debtors.

And do not lead us into temptation,

But deliver us from the _____ one.

For Yours is the _____ and the

_____ and the _____ forever. Amen.

Matthew 6:9–13 NKJV

Find the answers on page 191

Word Search

Can you find all the words?
Words may be forward, backward, or up-and-down.

BREAD   EARTH   HEAVEN   NEED

DAILY   FATHER   HOLY   PRAYER

DOOR   FORGIVE   KINGDOM   TEMPTATION

Q N E E D L W D T F G S R T
G H K M N B R E A D H Q K B D D
G B H Q W D S N M O D G N I K N A B
D F G W Q P R A Y E R B W M T L T I D B
N E V A E H H M R G R H D B K T X L T N
F M F O R G I V E W Q O M N K X T Y V T
D S R R O O D B C D W L N B G R W B X C
F A T H E R N B D Q Y Q E A R T H W
G T M V L R C K E E D N W S B M
N T E M P T A T I O N R S M

Find the answers on page 192

Jesus went to a quiet garden and prayed to God about all that was about to happen to Him.

Jesus taught people about God.
He told them to love each other and be kind.

Jesus and Nicodemus

Some Jewish leaders wanted to be saved through obeying the law, but Jesus had a different message. A Jewish leader named Nicodemus knew there was something special about Jesus, and had some questions for Him.

WHAT DO YOU KNOW ABOUT NICODEMUS?

1. When did Nicodemus talk to Jesus?
(John 3:2)

a) early in the morning
b) at noon
c) at suppertime
d) at night

2. What did Nicodemus already believe about Jesus? (John 3:2)

a) that His mother was Mary
b) that He was sent from God
c) that He could perform miracles
d) that He had many followers

3. What did Jesus tell Nicodemus?
(John 3:3)

a) that everyone must be baptized
b) that everyone must become a disciple
c) that everyone must be born again
d) that everyone must go to church

4. How did Nicodemus react to Jesus's words? (John 3:4, 9)

a) he walked away
b) he laughed
c) he became angry
d) he asked questions

5. What did Jesus explain to Nicodemus?
(John 3:16)

a) he had to obey the law to be saved
b) he had to be a missionary to be saved
c) he had to believe in Jesus to be saved
d) he had to read the Bible to be saved

6. Why did God send Jesus into the world?
(John 3:16)

a) so Jesus could do miracles
b) so Jesus could heal the sick
c) so Jesus could teach us to be kind
d) because God loves us so much

7. What did Jesus say about the things He taught people? (John 7:16)

a) "My teaching comes from God, who sent Me"
b) "My teaching comes from the law"
c) "My teaching comes from angels"
d) "My teaching comes from a dream"

8. What did Nicodemus say when some of the Jewish leaders wanted to arrest Jesus? (John 7:50–51)

a) "Jesus has done nothing wrong"
b) "Let Jesus go home"
c) "Our law says we must first find out what He has done"
d) "You guys are bullies"

Find the answers on page 192

Fill in the Blanks

See if you can fill in the words to this Bible verse without looking it up. After you finish, check the verse to see if your words are correct.

For _____ so _____ the world that

he _____ his one and only _____,

that whoever _____

in him shall _____ perish

but have _____ _____."

John 3:16 NIV

Word Search

Can you find all the words?
Words may be forward, backward, or up-and-down.

JESUS   BORN   SAVED

LEADERS   BELIEVE   JEWISH

LOVE   QUESTIONS   NIGHT

NICODEMUS   AGAIN   WORLD

```
H M D G N I C O D E M U S N C M S L
Q R W R L T I G N I G H T Q K L N O
H G S H S I W E J N B T Y N S W T V
P W B E L I E V E M W N R O B H L E
B V N G A G A I N T H S A V E D K L
R S S R E D A E L M W Q S T O N S H
M D L P N S Q U E S T I O N S N G T
B V K L J E S U S N M W O R L D G F
```

Find the answers on page 192

Jesus rode a donkey into the city of Jerusalem.
Many people were going there to celebrate a feast.

Jesus washed His disciples' feet.
Then they shared a special dinner together.

Jesus and the Cross

God sent Jesus to the world to take away our sins. He came not just for the Israelites, but for all people. When He died on the cross, Jesus took the punishment we deserved. If we believe in Him, we can be with God forever.

WHAT DO YOU KNOW ABOUT JESUS'S DEATH AND RESURRECTION?

1. **Where was Jesus praying when Judas brought enemies to arrest Him?**
   (Matthew 26:36)

   a) the garden of Gethsemane
   b) the temple court
   c) the pool of Siloam
   d) the gate of Jerusalem

2. **Who was the Roman governor that Jesus was taken to?** (John 18:28–29)

   a) Caesar
   b) Herod
   c) Pilate
   d) Caiaphas

3. **What did the governor tell the Jews after he talked to Jesus?** (John 18:38)

   a) that Jesus was a criminal
   b) that he found no guilt in Jesus
   c) that Jesus should be crucified
   d) that Jesus should be thrown in prison

4. **What did Pilate want to do after ordering Jesus to be beaten?**
   (John 19:12)

   a) put Him in prison
   b) release Him
   c) send Him back to the chief priest
   d) crucify Him

5. **What did Pilate have written on a sign that was nailed to Jesus's cross?**
   (John 19:19)

   a) "Behold, the Lamb of God"
   b) "A Criminal from Nazareth"
   c) "Guilty"
   d) "Jesus of Nazareth, the King of the Jews"

6. **Which two men buried Jesus after He died?** (John 19:38–39)

   a) Simon of Cyrene and Judas
   b) Peter and John
   c) Saul of Tarsus and Barnabas
   d) Joseph of Arimathea and Nicodemus

7. **Who asked Mary Magdalene why she was crying near Jesus's tomb?**
   (John 20:11–13)

   a) two angels
   b) Peter and John
   c) the gardener
   d) Pilate

8. **When Mary realized that Jesus had come back from the dead, what did she say to Him?** (John 20:15–18)

   a) "Hallelujah!"
   b) "My Lord!"
   c) "Rabboni!" (which means "Teacher!")
   d) "You're alive!"

Find the answers on page 192

Jesus died on the cross to save us from our sins.
Everyone who believes in Jesus
will live with Him in heaven.

Word Search

Can you find all the words?
Words may be forward, backward, or up-and-down.

```
              U B L A R H P J
              Z E N O T S N M
              R L Y J A S H E
              N S I L V E R L
    K E A R T H Q U A K E O T R Q K U H
    P X G N S S O R C H M B T W I L M E
    Y M C I H S O W N W L B E R Y K A J
    L V P R I E S T S H U E L S N I T O
    I T E O B A I F L E T R U T W S M C
    Q S P A W O H G N Q R S F S H U T W
              B W O M E N J C
              C Z A N G E L I
              F D C R O W N T
              M H U B W O D S
              E Q G U A R D H
              X T O M B R L K
              H A N D W E G O
              V Y E P O K N W
              G D A R K L O M
              E J U S M R Q Y
```

ANGEL

CROSS

CROWN

DARK

EARTHQUAKE

GUARD

PRIESTS

ROBBERS

SILVER

STONE

TOMB

WOMEN

Find the answers on page 193

Crossword Puzzle

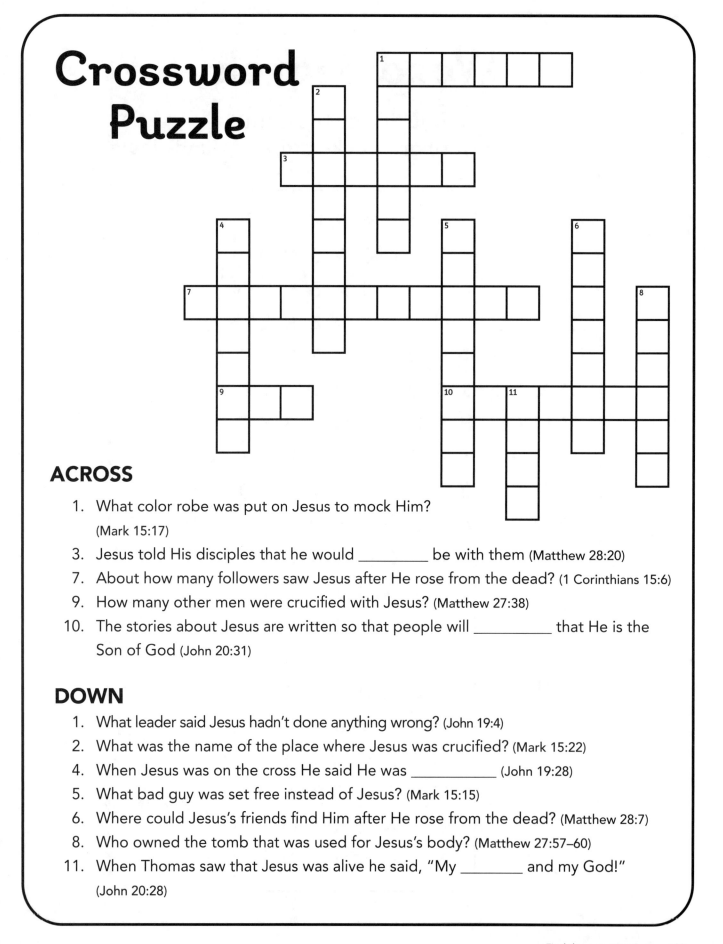

ACROSS

1. What color robe was put on Jesus to mock Him?
(Mark 15:17)
3. Jesus told His disciples that he would _____ be with them (Matthew 28:20)
7. About how many followers saw Jesus after He rose from the dead? (1 Corinthians 15:6)
9. How many other men were crucified with Jesus? (Matthew 27:38)
10. The stories about Jesus are written so that people will _____ that He is the Son of God (John 20:31)

DOWN

1. What leader said Jesus hadn't done anything wrong? (John 19:4)
2. What was the name of the place where Jesus was crucified? (Mark 15:22)
4. When Jesus was on the cross He said He was _____ (John 19:28)
5. What bad guy was set free instead of Jesus? (Mark 15:15)
6. Where could Jesus's friends find Him after He rose from the dead? (Matthew 28:7)
8. Who owned the tomb that was used for Jesus's body? (Matthew 27:57–60)
11. When Thomas saw that Jesus was alive he said, "My _____ and my God!"
(John 20:28)

Find the answers on page 193

Finish the Picture

Using the grid provided, draw the reflection
of the image shown to complete the picture.

A few days later, some women went to the tomb. The stone was rolled away and Jesus was not there.

Jesus Is Alive

After Jesus rose from the dead, He appeared to many people. Even though Jesus had predicted His resurrection, some people were still surprised to see Him.

WHAT DO YOU KNOW ABOUT THE TIMES WHEN JESUS APPEARED TO PEOPLE AFTER HE ROSE FROM THE DEAD?

1. **On the day Jesus came back to life, two men were walking along a road. Where were they going?** (Luke 24:13)

   a) Jerusalem
   b) Bethany
   c) Emmaus
   d) Jericho

2. **Who came along and walked with them?** (Luke 24:15)

   a) Peter
   b) Andrew
   c) Philip
   d) Jesus

3. **When did the two men recognize the person who had been walking with them?** (Luke 24:30–31)

   a) when they stopped to rest
   b) when they ate bread together
   c) when they told each other their names
   d) when they said goodbye

4. **Where were the disciples when Jesus first appeared to them?** (John 20:19)

   a) at the Sea of Galilee
   b) at the temple
   c) in a locked room
   d) at Peter's house

5. **What happened when Peter and some of the other disciples went fishing?** (John 21:3)

   a) they caught a shark
   b) they tore their nets
   c) a big storm rocked their boat
   d) they caught nothing

6. **What did Jesus, who was standing on the shore, tell them to do?** (John 21:6)

   a) throw their nets on the right side of the boat
   b) go out farther into the sea
   c) come to shore right away
   d) take a nap

7. **What did Jesus say to the disciples after they caught a net full of fish?** (John 21:12)

   a) "Keep fishing."
   b) "Let's go home."
   c) "Who's hungry?"
   d) "Come and have breakfast."

8. **What question did Jesus ask Peter three times?** (John 21:15–17)

   a) "Will you follow me?"
   b) "Do you love me?"
   c) "Are you tired?"
   d) "Do you like to fish?"

Find the answers on page 193

Three days later
Jesus rose from the dead.
He spent time with the disciples
and went back to heaven.

Coded Message

What was Mary Magdalene's message to the disciples?
Use the key below to match the symbols
to letters to break the code.

_ _ _ _ _   _ _   _ _ _ _ _!
(JESUS IS ALIVE!)

❁	⊛	✛	❄	❅	◆	✳	★	✺	✪	✳	●	○
A	B	C	D	E	F	G	H	I	J	K	L	M

■	◻	▢	✳	✲	▲	▼	◆	❖	◗	✳	❙	✺
N	O	P	Q	R	S	T	U	V	W	X	Y	Z

Find the answers on page 193

The women were so excited,
they ran to tell their friends.

Word Search

Can you find all the words?
Words may be forward or backward.

THOMAS   PETER   FISHING   BREAKFAST

LOVE   DOUBT   CLEOPAS   EMMAUS

LOCKED   APPEAR   ROAD   MEN

```
          W D R H U
        O A M E N H G L K
      S T P E T E R D R O A D K
      V Q S D S A M O H T H L O V E
    G H F I S H I N G T H L O C K E D
    C L C L E O P A S K D L H B T K L
    M S U A M M E T H A P P E A R H P
    K B R E A K F A S T K N B G R
      D O U B T K G R D T W D N
        J F D R F D C B N M P
          P J L E Y O I
```

Find the answers on page 194

Maze

Follow the maze to connect Peter to the shore where Jesus is waiting with breakfast.

Find the answers on page 194

Crossword Puzzle

ACROSS

1. Who asked Jesus to show the disciples the Father? (John 14:8)
3. The way to the Father (John 14:6)
6. Jesus told His disciples things that were going to happen so they would _____ (John 14:29)
8. The Helper the Father sent is the Spirit of _____ (John 14:16–17)
9. Jesus told His disciples He would not _____ them as orphans (John 14:18)
11. Jesus promised that He is _____ back (John 14:28)
12. Whoever believes in Jesus will do great _____ (John 14:12)

DOWN

2. Jesus went to prepare a place for His followers at His Father's _____ (John 14:2)
4. Jesus promised the Holy Spirit would teach the disciples _____ (John 14:26)
5. Anyone who has seen Jesus has also seen whom? (John 14:9)
7. Jesus said if we _____ Him we will keep His commands (John 14:15)
10. There are many _____ in the Father's house (John 14:2)

Find the answers on page 194

The Holy Spirit

After Jesus went back to heaven, the Holy Spirit came to the disciples. He helped them do things they could not do before. The Holy Spirit was the Helper Jesus had promised. The Holy Spirit is our helper too.

WHAT DO YOU KNOW ABOUT THE HOLY SPIRIT?

1. **What did Jesus say the disciples would receive from the Holy Spirit?** (Acts 1:8)

   a) doves
   b) power
   c) money
   d) friends

2. **When the Holy Spirit came into the room where the disciples were, what did it sound like?** (Acts 2:2)

   a) a freight train
   b) a bus
   c) a strong wind
   d) a lion's roar

3. **What did the disciples see above each others' heads when they received the Holy Spirit?** (Acts 2:3)

   a) small flames of fire
   b) golden crowns
   c) white doves
   d) butterflies

4. **What ability did the Holy Spirit give to the believers?** (Acts 2:4)

   a) they could run fast
   b) they could go without eating
   c) they could fly
   d) they could speak in different languages

5. **What were the other people talking about after they received the Holy Spirit?** (Acts 2:11)

   a) Roman leaders
   b) the great wonders of God
   c) the Olympics
   d) the weather

6. **Which disciple tried to explain to the people what was happening?** (Acts 2:14)

   a) James
   b) Matthew
   c) Peter
   d) John

7. **How could the other people in the crowd receive the Holy Spirit?** (Acts 2:38)

   a) they could ask the disciples
   b) they could go to the Temple
   c) they could climb the Mount of Olives
   d) they could turn away from their sins and be baptized

8. **What does the Holy Spirit do when we pray?** (Romans 8:26)

   a) He keeps us awake
   b) He sings
   c) He prays to God for us
   d) He flies around heaven

Find the answers on page 194

Word Search

Can you find all the words?
Words may be forward, backward, or diagonal.

CHRISTIAN   HELPER   POWER

DISCIPLES   HOLY   SPIRIT

FLAMES   JESUS   TRUTH

FRIENDS   LANGUAGE   WIND

```
D H K M R H T U R T S N V J E S U S Q W
G W K L D S Z W C B P O W E R T L S Z M
Q M I K N D S E M A L F M W H P T N T Q
B D H N Q W F R I E N D S D W O P L N V
D X C B D M K S P I R I T H W L L B V S
W B Q D I S C I P L E S W N Q B H Y N L
R E P L E H M K H C H R I S T I A N N B
M N B L A N G U A G E M W P T L J S Z Q
```

Find the answers on page 195

Decode the Message

Using the key, decode the message.

Find the answers on page 195

KEY	
1 = H	14 = W
2 = E	15 = X
3 = A	16 = K
4 = J	17 = I
5 = P	18 = D
6 = B	19 = N
7 = M	20 = T
8 = F	21 = L
9 = S	22 = V
10 = Z	23 = C
11 = Q	24 = R
12 = O	25 = G
13 = Y	26 = U

—— —— ——   —— —— —— ——
20   1   2   1 12 21 13

—— —— —— —— —— ——
9   5   17 24 17 20

—— ——   —— —— ——
17   9   12 26 24

—— —— —— —— —— —— .
1   2 21   5   2 24

Crossword Puzzle

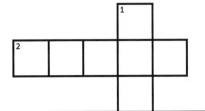

ACROSS

2. What did the Holy Spirit give to the disciples? (Acts 1:8)

3. The Holy Spirit is also called the Spirit of _____ (John 16:13)

8. People were surprised to hear the disciples speaking in different _____ (Acts 2:8)

10. What Old Testament prophet said that the Holy Spirit would come? (Acts 2:16–17)

11. When we pray, the Holy Spirit _____ for us (Romans 8:26)

12. The day the Holy Spirit came is called _____ (Acts 2:1)

DOWN

1. Who told the disciples they would receive a Helper? (John 14:9–17)
4. Who lives within us when we become Christians? (2 Timothy 1:14)
5. What did it sound like when the Holy Spirit came into the room? (Acts 2:2)
6. Where did Jesus go before the Holy Spirit came to earth? (Acts 1:11)
7. What appeared over the heads of the disciples when the Holy Spirit came? (Acts 2:3)
9. What did Jesus call His disciples when He knew He would soon be leaving them? (John 15:15)

Find the answers on page 195

Make as many words as you can out of the letters in
Holy Spirit

Word Search

Can you find all the words?
Words may be forward, backward, or up-and-down.

HOLY SPIRIT   PREPARE   HELPER

PEACE   WORKS   COMING

ROOMS   FATHER   WAY

HOUSE   TEACH   COMMANDS

```
H C O M M A N D S G
P C B E C A E P K M W A Y N
R H P R P R E P A R E D M W
O H S K R O W T H N H Y B D
O T H F A T H E R G O G N R
M K C H T E A C H K U T H G
S M H E L P E R D Q S H N M
C M G N I M O C B R E C B W
D W Q H O L Y S P I R I T Q
```

Find the answers on page 195

Crossword Puzzle

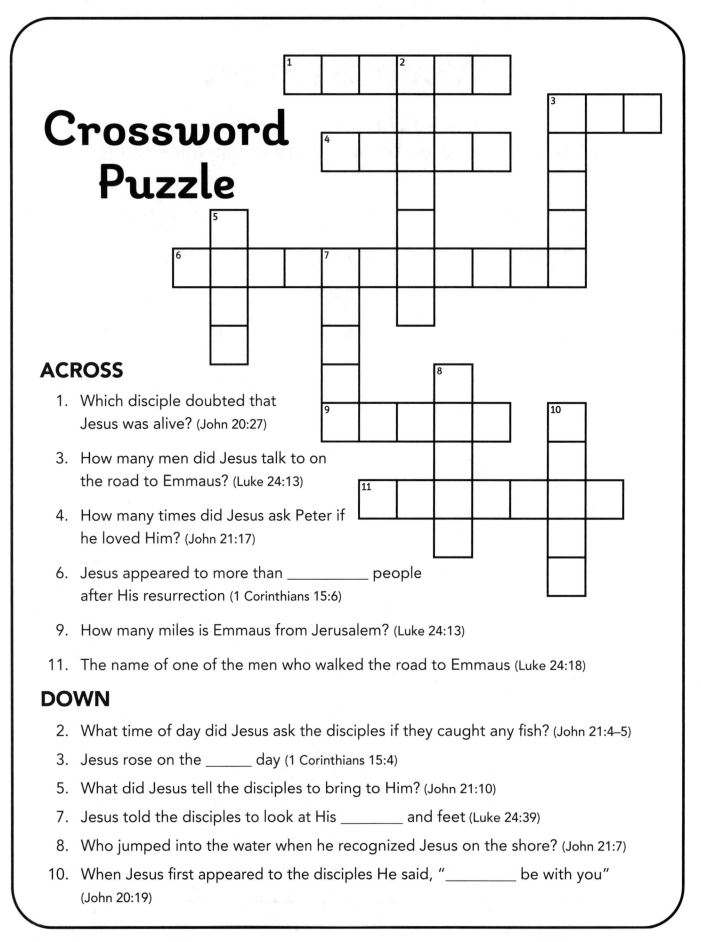

ACROSS

1. Which disciple doubted that Jesus was alive? (John 20:27)

3. How many men did Jesus talk to on the road to Emmaus? (Luke 24:13)

4. How many times did Jesus ask Peter if he loved Him? (John 21:17)

6. Jesus appeared to more than _____ people after His resurrection (1 Corinthians 15:6)

9. How many miles is Emmaus from Jerusalem? (Luke 24:13)

11. The name of one of the men who walked the road to Emmaus (Luke 24:18)

DOWN

2. What time of day did Jesus ask the disciples if they caught any fish? (John 21:4–5)

3. Jesus rose on the _____ day (1 Corinthians 15:4)

5. What did Jesus tell the disciples to bring to Him? (John 21:10)

7. Jesus told the disciples to look at His _____ and feet (Luke 24:39)

8. Who jumped into the water when he recognized Jesus on the shore? (John 21:7)

10. When Jesus first appeared to the disciples He said, "_____ be with you" (John 20:19)

Find the answers on page 196

A New Follower

One of the greatest followers of Jesus was a man who at first hated Christians. God had a very special plan for this man to take the good news to people in different parts of the world. We can read his story and his teachings through his writings in the New Testament.

WHAT DO YOU KNOW ABOUT A VERY SPECIAL FOLLOWER OF JESUS AND THE FIRST MISSIONARIES?

1. **What did a proud Pharisee named Saul do to the early Christians?** (Acts 8:3)

    a) he stole their donkeys
    b) he burned their homes
    c) he made fun of them in the streets
    d) he threw them in prison

2. **What did God tell Ananias to do?** (Acts 9:10–15)

    a) arrest Saul to keep him from attacking the Christians
    b) baptize Saul in the Jordan River
    c) heal Saul's blindness so he could become a great missionary
    d) speak to Saul on the road to Damascus

3. **What was Saul's name changed to?** (Acts 13:9)

    a) Paul
    b) Peter
    c) Simeon
    d) Samuel

4. **Who was the first to travel with Paul on his missionary journeys?** (Acts 12:25)

    a) Cornelius
    b) Thomas
    c) Barnabas
    d) Lazarus

5. **Which of these things did *not* happen to Paul during his missionary travels?** (2 Corinthians 11:25)

    a) he was beaten with rods
    b) he was crucified
    c) he was stoned
    d) he was shipwrecked three times

6. **Paul said he counted everything as a loss compared to what?** (Philippians 3:8)

    a) being a Pharisee
    b) preaching the good news
    c) obeying the Ten Commandments
    d) knowing Jesus Christ

7. **After being rich and poor, powerful and weak, what did Paul learn?** (Philippians 4:12–13)

    a) "I am better because of it"
    b) "I am happier with less"
    c) "I can do all things through Christ who gives me strength"
    d) "I can rely on my own strength"

8. **Who did Paul say is the image of the invisible God?** (Colossians 1:13–15)

    a) the disciples
    b) Jesus, God's Son
    c) the church
    d) the angels

Find the answers on page 196

The disciples couldn't stop telling people about Jesus. The church grew and grew.

Maze

Help the disciples spread the
gospel to the whole world!

Find the answers on page 196

Word Art

Color the letters and words about some of the books in the New Testament.

The total number of books in the New Testament is _____ .

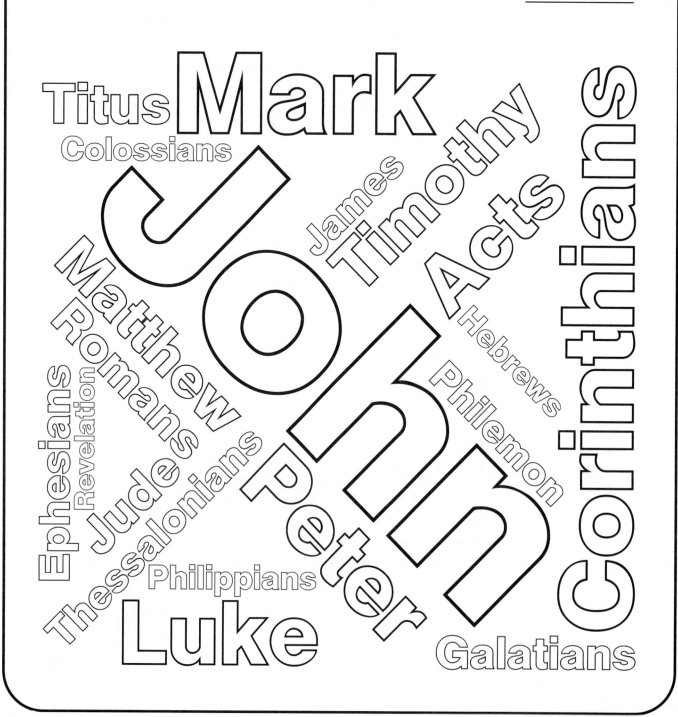

Find the answers on page 196

Just like Jesus's first followers, we can tell others the good news about Him.

Love

Jesus came to earth to show us how much God loves us. He taught people how to love God and how to love each other. God used some of Jesus's followers to write about love in the Bible so we can learn about God's love too.

WHAT DO YOU KNOW ABOUT WHAT THE BIBLE SAYS ABOUT LOVE?

1. **What did Jesus say is the first great commandment?** (Matthew 22:37–38)

   a) obey your parents

   b) eat your vegetables

   c) don't tell lies

   d) love God with all your heart, soul, and mind

2. **What did Jesus say is the second great commandment?** (Matthew 22:39)

   a) go to church every week

   b) listen to Christian music

   c) love your neighbor as yourself

   d) drink plenty of water

3. **What are people like if they do not have love?** (1 Corinthians 13:1)

   a) a barking dog

   b) a clanging cymbal

   c) a honking horn

   d) a wailing siren

4. **Which of the following words describe what love is?** (1 Corinthians 13:4)

   a) patient and kind

   b) nice and clean

   c) soft and warm

   d) sweet and sour

5. **Where does the Bible say love comes from?** (1 John 4:7)

   a) our grandparents

   b) our parents

   c) the angels

   d) God

6. **What does God call us because He loves us so much?** (1 John 3:1)

   a) Christians

   b) the church

   c) His children

   d) His helpers

7. **What should we do because God loves us?** (1 John 4:11)

   a) jump up and down

   b) shout "Amen!"

   c) love other people

   d) sit still and fold our hands

8. **How long will God's love last?** (Psalm 136:1)

   a) as long as we obey Him

   b) as long as we love Him

   c) as long as we are good

   d) forever

Find the answers on page 196

Connect the Dots

Connect the dots below to see a very important message!

Jesus loves you with all of His heart! He said, "Let the little children come to me."

Crossword Puzzle

ACROSS

1. One way to show our love is to _____ others (Ephesians 4:32)
3. Jesus tells us to love our _____ (Matthew 22:39)
6. What can separate us from God's love? (see Romans 8:38–39)
9. Who died for us because of God's love? (Romans 5:8)
10. What is greater than faith and hope? (1 Corinthians 13:13)
11. We love others because God loves _____ (1 John 4:19)

DOWN

1. Loving God is the _____ great commandment (Matthew 22:37–38)
2. Who is love? (1 John 4:16)
4. God's love fills the _____ (Psalm 33:5)
5. What can we read to learn about God's love?
7. Because God loves us He forgives our ____ (1 John 1:9)
8. We should love God with all our _____ (Deuteronomy 6:5)

Find the answers on page 197

Word Search

Can you find all the words? Words may be forward or backward.

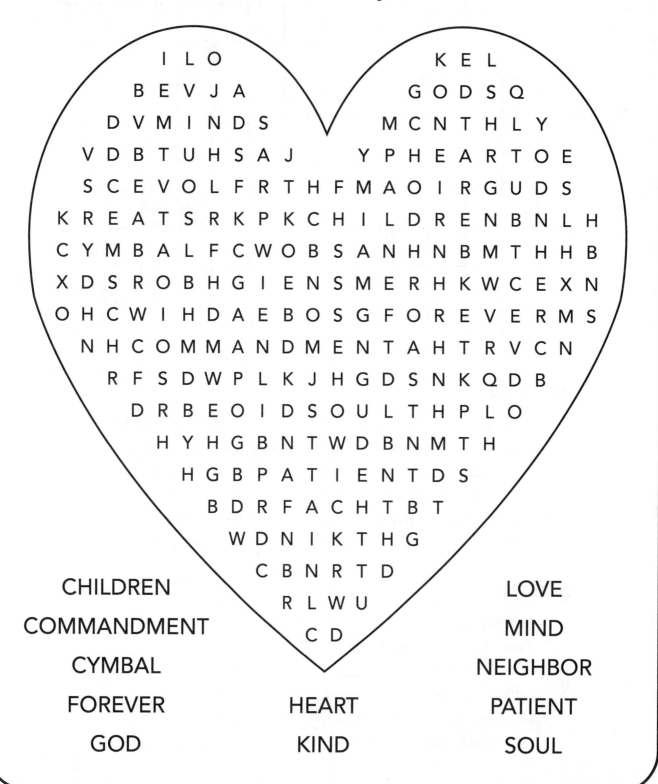

```
        I L O                     K E L
      B E V J A               G O D S Q
    D V M I N D S           M C N T H L Y
  V D B T U H S A J       Y P H E A R T O E
  S C E V O L F R T H F M A O I R G U D S
K R E A T S R K P K C H I L D R E N B N L H
C Y M B A L F C W O B S A N H N B M T H H B
X D S R O B H G I E N S M E R H K W C E X N
O H C W I H D A E B O S G F O R E V E R M S
N H C O M M A N D M E N T A H T R V C N
  R F S D W P L K J H G D S N K Q D B
    D R B E O I D S O U L T H P L O
      H Y H G B N T W D B N M T H
        H G B P A T I E N T D S
          B D R F A C H T B T
            W D N I K T H G
              C B N R T D
                R L W U
                  C D
```

CHILDREN

COMMANDMENT

CYMBAL

FOREVER

GOD

HEART

KIND

LOVE

MIND

NEIGHBOR

PATIENT

SOUL

Find the answers on page 197

The Bible is God's word to us. You can
learn more about God by reading your Bible.

Fill in the Blank

What will people who follow Jesus do?
Read John 13:35 (ERV).
Use the words below to fill in the blanks.

"All _ _ _ _ _ _ will _ _ _ _

that _ _ _ are my _ _ _ _ _ _ _ _ _

if you _ _ _ _ each _ _ _ _ _ _."

- ❏ love
- ❏ know
- ❏ you
- ❏ followers
- ❏ other
- ❏ people

Fruit of the Spirit

Jesus promised that He would send His Holy Spirit to give power to His followers. With the Holy Spirit's strength, Christians would be able to face hard situations. The Holy Spirit gives Christians gifts—called "fruit"—to help them obey God.

WHAT DO YOU KNOW ABOUT THE FRUIT OF THE SPIRIT?

1. **How many good things are listed as the fruit of the Spirit?**
   (Galatians 5:22–23)

   a) three
   b) seven
   c) nine
   d) twelve

2. **Which of these is not part of the fruit of the Spirit?** (Galatians 5:22–23)

   a) joy
   b) selfishness
   c) love
   d) self-control

3. **Which of these is not listed as the fruit of the Spirit?** (Galatians 5:22–23)

   a) giving money to church
   b) peace
   c) patience
   d) kindness

4. **The apostle Paul says there is no _____ that says the fruit of the Spirit is wrong.** (Galatians 5:22–23)

   a) book
   b) person
   c) law
   d) king

5. **What is the opposite of living life by God's Spirit?** (Galatians 5:16–17)

   a) doing whatever we want, including sin
   b) doing what our parents tell us to do
   c) helping a friend who is hurt
   d) being a good listener

6. **When we live by the Spirit, what does Paul say we shouldn't be?**
   (Galatians 5:26)

   a) sleepy
   b) hyper
   c) frustrated
   d) conceited, or proud

7. **We have life in the Spirit because Jesus made us _____.** (Galatians 5:1)

   a) alive
   b) free
   c) clean
   d) happy

8. **What does Paul say we should use our freedom in the Spirit for?**
   (Galatians 5:13)

   a) making lots of money
   b) traveling the world
   c) singing solos at church
   d) serving each other, in love

Find the answers on page 197

Color by Number

How many hidden fruits can you find?

1	2	3	4	5	6	7
RED	ORANGE	YELLOW	GREEN	PURPLE	BROWN	BLACK

Word Search

Can you find all the words?
Words may be forward, backward, or up-and-down.

FAITHFULNESS   GOODNESS   PATIENCE

FREE   JOY   PEACE

FRUIT   KINDNESS   SELF-CONTROL

GENTLENESS   LOVE   SPIRIT

```
F S R         N K L
K F R U I T H G N L B
G T S S E N D O O G H N B
F R F A I T H F U L N E S S M
H L W K V M L H K P E A C E N L K
Y O J M G E N T L E N E S S M W Q
K V Q N R F G N P A T I E N C E M
S E L F C O N T R O L K N D J S N
G H D K T N D N V T T J K O G
T K I N D N E S S D V N Y
H G B N L J E E R F Q
N S P I R I T W S
```

Find the answers on page 197

Crossword Puzzle

ACROSS

1. You can shine for Jesus by doing _____ things (Matthew 5:16)
3. God's Spirit gives us ____ and love and self-control (2 Timothy 1:7)
4. Paul told Timothy that even though he was young, he could be an example because of his _____ (1 Timothy 4:12)
5. The last good thing listed in the fruit of the Spirit (Galatians 5:23)
7. Jesus said that a branch needs to be connected to the _____ to bear fruit (John 15:4)
9. Kind words are sweet like _____ (Proverbs 16:24)

DOWN

1. What kind of answer turns away anger? (Proverbs 15:1)
2. Paul said some people were trying to be right with God by living according to the _____ instead of the Spirit (Galatians 5:4)
3. What should control our hearts and minds? (Colossians 3:15)
5. We receive fruit from the _____ (Galatians 5:22)
6. The first good thing listed in the fruit of the Spirit (Galatians 5:22)
8. What does God fill us with when we follow His ways? (Psalm 16:11)

Find the answers on page 198

You can share God's
love by helping your friends.
When you help others,
you show them you care.

The Church

After Jesus went to heaven, His followers began to meet in homes to share meals, to pray together, and to talk about Jesus. This was the beginning of "going to church."

WHAT DO YOU KNOW ABOUT THE START OF THE CHURCH?

1. **What did the first Christians pray for as they spread the good news about Jesus?** (Acts 4:29)

   a) for things to go smoothly
   b) for the king to like them
   c) for boldness to speak without fear
   d) for the ability to perform miracles

2. **Who was trying to destroy the new church by putting Christians in prison?** (Acts 8:3)

   a) Simon Peter
   b) Barnabas
   c) Barabbas
   d) Saul

3. **Where were Jesus's followers first called "Christians"?** (Acts 11:26)

   a) Antioch
   b) Athens
   c) Jerusalem
   d) Ephesus

4. **When did Saul, later called Paul, become a Christian?** (Acts 9:3–5)

   a) after hearing Peter preach a sermon
   b) after he saw Jesus's empty tomb
   c) after seeing a bright light and hearing Jesus speak
   d) after he was swallowed by a whale

5. **Who were the first missionaries sent out by the church?** (Acts 13:2–3)

   a) James and John
   b) Barnabas and Saul
   c) Barabbas and Paul
   d) David and Goliath

6. **How far did Jesus tell His disciples to spread the good news?** (Acts 1:8)

   a) throughout Asia
   b) as far as Egypt
   c) around Galilee
   d) to the ends of the earth

7. **What is another name for the church?** (Colossians 1:18)

   a) a group of angels
   b) the sword of the Spirit
   c) the body of Christ
   d) the big white building with a steeple

8. **What does the Bible say the church is built from?** (Ephesians 2:19–22)

   a) bricks and mortar
   b) stone and marble
   c) prayers and songs
   d) all of God's people

Find the answers on page 198

Word Search

Can you find all the words?
Words may be forward, backward, or up-and-down.

ANTIOCH

BAPTIZE

BODY OF CHRIST

BOLDNESS

CHRISTIANS

CHURCH

CORNERSTONE

LETTERS

MISSIONARY

PREACH

SHARE

TEACHER

```
          H G
        R D T K
      H S H A R E
      R L E T T E R S
      T Q N H C A E R P K
  T H N G X R T C H R I S T I A N S K Q B
  E N S S E N D L O B H Z N H N K M N V A
  A R H D T C H C O R N E R S T O N E Q P
  C B M I S S I O N A R Y N H I G R S N T
  H T N R S H C R U H C W K T O S Q N C I
  E Q T R H S D M Q D F R H M C H C V B Z
  R H B O D Y O F C H R I S T H K H K T E
```

Find the answers on page 198

When we believe in Jesus,
the Holy Spirit helps
us to share God's love.

MATTHEW 22:39 ♡JULIE

Jesus Is Coming Back!

The Bible tells us that Jesus lived on earth a little more than thirty years before going back to heaven. But Jesus had told His followers that He would come back to earth someday. We don't know when Jesus is coming back, but we do know that He will.

WHAT DO YOU KNOW ABOUT JESUS COMING BACK?

1. **As Jesus was going to heaven, who told the disciples that Jesus would come back?** (Acts 1:10–11)
   a) Jesus's mother Mary
   b) the apostle Paul
   c) two men dressed in white
   d) Jewish leaders

2. **Who knows exactly when Jesus is going to return to earth?** (Mark 13:32)
   a) Christians
   b) Bible teachers
   c) the angels
   d) only God the Father

3. **Who is preparing a place for us in heaven?** (John 14:1–2)
   a) Abraham
   b) Simon Peter
   c) our great-great grandparents
   d) Jesus

4. **What should we do while we wait for Jesus to return?** (Galatians 6:9–10)
   a) play video games
   b) do good things for others
   c) listen to music
   d) watch TV

5. **Who will see Jesus when He returns?** (Revelation 1:7)
   a) missionaries
   b) pastors
   c) everyone who's awake at the time
   d) everyone

6. **What must happen before Jesus returns?** (Matthew 24:14)
   a) everyone needs to be baptized
   b) everyone will become a missionary
   c) everyone should read the Bible
   d) the good news of God's kingdom must be preached to all nations

7. **What will happen to God's children when Jesus returns?** (1 John 3:2)
   a) they will become like Jesus
   b) they will become like angels
   c) they will be afraid
   d) they will stay on earth

8. **What did Jesus say about His return?** (Revelation 22:20)
   a) He is coming soon
   b) He is coming in power
   c) He is going to fix up the mess
   d) He will swoop down like an eagle

Find the answers on page 198

Crossword Puzzle

ACROSS

1. From what direction did the prophet Ezekiel say Jesus will return? (Ezekiel 43:1–2)

3. When Jesus comes back, Christians will be taken up into the _____ (1 Thessalonians 4:17)

5. Jesus will use His _____ to change our bodies to be like His (Philippians 3:21)

7. When Jesus comes from heaven it will be like _____ flashing in the sky (Matthew 24:27)

8. When Jesus returns for His people, He will wipe away every _____ from their eyes (Revelation 21:4)

11. How long will we be with Jesus after he returns? (1 Thessalonians 4:17)

12. Jesus said He will make everything _____ (Revelation 21:5)

DOWN

2. What instrument will sound when Jesus returns? (Matthew 24:31)

4. Who will be coming with Jesus when He returns? (Matthew 16:27)

6. What color were the clothes of the men who told the disciples Jesus would come back? (Acts 1:10–11)

9. When Jesus returns, He will _____ us for the good things we have done (Revelation 22:12)

10. Where is our true homeland? (Philippians 3:20)

Find the answers on page 199

Word Search

Can you find all the words?
Words may be forward, backward, or up-and-down.

EAST   FATHER   PREPARE   RULE

EVERYONE   HEAVEN   RETURN   SOMEDAY

EZEKIEL   JESUS   REVELATION   WAIT

```
H N D W R T J E S U S T K S Z E Q N B W
Y A D E M O S L H T J C B R F A H R S A
K B V D R E T U R N H R T J R S K L M I
F A T H E R X N P H N E Z N J T D R B T
N B H D K N E V A E H L G Z F N J U N R
D M E V E R Y O N E N T B S Y P L L N T
M L E I K E Z E M W B P L Z F H N E V R
N D G H P R E P A R E K N W L T H N C T
N B H R D G C B K L R E V E L A T I O N
```

Find the answers on page 199

John Tells Us About Heaven

Many people were becoming Christians, and the religious leaders treated Jesus's followers badly. The disciple John was sent away to try to keep him from sharing the good news. But God's plans were bigger. God showed John what heaven is like, and he wrote down what he saw for us!

WHAT DO YOU KNOW ABOUT THE BIBLE?

1. **Where did John write the book of Revelation?** (Revelation 1:9)

   a) the Valley of Lebanon
   b) the Island of Patmos
   c) the Lake of Gennesaret
   d) the Tower of Babel

2. **What did John say about Jesus?** (Revelation 1:7)

   a) "He is in Galilee"
   b) "He is going to Jerusalem"
   c) "He is staying in heaven forever"
   d) "He is coming with the clouds"

3. **What sound did John hear?** (Revelation 1:10)

   a) a loud voice that sounded like a trumpet
   b) a loud boom that sounded like a drum
   c) a loud noise that sounded like a train
   d) a loud choir singing songs

4. **What was John told to do?** (Revelation 1:11)

   a) take pictures of what he saw
   b) pay close attention to what he saw
   c) write down what he saw
   d) close his eyes

5. **How was John allowed to see into heaven?** (Revelation 4:1)

   a) through a crack in the floor
   b) through a window
   c) through a door
   d) through a telescope

6. **What was around the throne that John saw in heaven?** (Revelation 4:3)

   a) a tree
   b) a rainbow
   c) a cloud
   d) a colorful window

7. **What does Revelation 22:5 say we will not need in heaven?**

   a) food and water
   b) toys and books
   c) light from a lamp or the sun
   d) pianos and organs

8. **What important message did Jesus tell John?** (Revelation 22:20)

   a) "I am your Lord"
   b) "I created you"
   c) "I am your Shepherd"
   d) "I am coming soon!"

Find the answers on page 199

Word Search

Can you find all the words?
Words may be forward, backward, up-and-down, or diagonal.

RAINBOW   PATMOS   JOHN   REVELATION

CLOUDS   SOON   ISLAND   HEAVEN

LIGHT   TRUMPET   THRONE   VOICE

```
        C J          I H
      A J L A C B O R D C K
    E A J Y A O D T Y E L P A J Y
  N I R O E V B U L A V E I R H S A
  M S U H S O O N D P E A W G U L K
  C U L S N L I E D T S L R O I H N E
  H E A V E N C W A N L A T B E G T
  I T N O H K E N O R H T B N Z R A
  N D S P A T M O S H I T I E N
    A W S G I L U M O M A A
      T R U M P E T N S R A
        C S A     H O L
```

Find the answers on page 199

Finish the Picture

Complete the scene by drawing angels rejoicing in heaven like John saw in the book of Revelation.

Make as many words as you can out of the letters in

Revelation

_____   _____

_____   _____

_____   _____

_____   _____

_____   _____

_____   _____

_____   _____

_____   _____

_____   _____

We can praise Jesus every day
and thank Him for His wonderful love.

Fill in the Blank

Read what Jesus said in John 8:12.
Use the words below to fill in the blanks.

- ❑ darkness
- ❑ me
- ❑ light
- ❑ life
- ❑ world
- ❑ walk

"I am the __ __ __ __ __ of the

__ __ __ __ __.

Whoever follows __ __ will never

__ __ __ __ in

__ __ __ __ __ __ __ __ __,

but will have the light of

__ __ __ __."

I give you a new command. _____ one another.
You must _____ one another,
just as I have _____ you.

John 13:34

ANSWER KEY

PAGE 3	PAGE 4

QUIZ 1

1. C

2. A

3. B

4. C

5. B

6. D

7. C

8. D

```
W Y M T C R D I S C I P L E S M W V H Q
X M W M P D R T I K P T N L U K E C Y P
Y Q M D O M T X I R L T I M O R F Q R J
B C W M P S X B T V T L I N V C R W S E
I W X Q Z B E L P C V V T S B R Y P M S
B F K B W Q D S Q D S Z R U Q O L L I U
L K X M B D B P P K C G V G O D L T T S
E F R H D M N T T J B B D M L O Q X L R
L K T M B A U T H O R K L N M P B D R H
K T B Q N J W M H R B S N B Q M B X S F
W T E S T A M E N T W L T N P X K H C P
M P R O P H E T S M M N X T L T P N D A
Q T K N W S T Q P S A L M S D C H F Q U
K X V F M G D B K L R T S M B O O K S L
```

ANSWER KEY

PAGE 6

39

PAGE 8

QUIZ 2

1. C
2. B
3. C
4. D
5. B
6. A
7. D
8. C

PAGE 9

```
        H
        E                        G
    E A R T H                    E
        V          N I G H T     N
        E V E                    E
        N ■ D                    S E A
        S   E                    I
        A N I M A L S            S
        D          L            I
    C R E A T E    I            G O D
        M          G            H
                   H            T
                   T
```

PAGE 10

```
      E C P K L S R B P N
    S Q P E O P L E M N X Z
    G O O D P M S S T A R S D L
    R T Q C T M Q B C S N S M T T H
  Y T W F T G A R D E N P X M R R T M
  T P L C X A N I M A L S X W E Q V T
  K N L G T D M O O N T R L T E X Z R
  W A T E R Q H G N M P L K W S F X C
  T C X L M P L A N T S T B B W T R Y
  R T L I G H T S D C T I I Z X S
    T N Q V X Z S Q D T R R K D
    F G B H H U T Y L P D C
    O B N H N Z H B D S
```

PAGE 11

QUIZ 3

1. D
2. A
3. B
4. C
5. C
6. D
7. C
8. D

PAGE 13

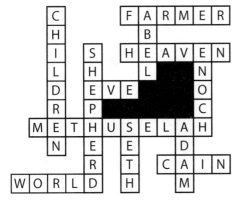

PAGE 15

```
G A D M A S D F K L P O C L O T H E S
A N O I H W A B N I W E B T S E M O I
R F S S E N E V I G R O F L A B S T K
D A N L N S W E L T L Y J E T D H O T
E L A E H L T I N S E L E O W I A H U
N M K Y I D R Y E A L O D M H S U M H
L T E M P T A T I O N M A S T O E D S
E M N I E K M R L V G C U N M B T H A
S O W L H I D E U F I T N E V E D E R
I T H M U A S E B R C K A W I Y B A O
A O S N C E I H A F R U I T V E H O N
```

PAGE 16

GENESIS

PAGE 18

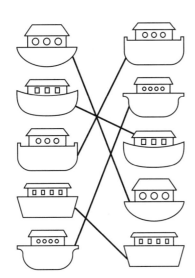

PAGE 19

QUIZ 4

1. C

2. A

3. D

4. D

5. C

6. B

7. C

8. B

ANSWER KEY

PAGE 21

```
H D S M N O A H K L O S H
  M E H S C G M S C D G R A
    F L O O D H T G H K D E M
M B N B M E W D J A P H E T H Q W K B X Z
A R Q K M W B P R O M I S E K B R D L O H
R H D G R T I S A A C B N M S C S A R A H
K B D Q D L L P A B R A H A M T P L X N T
K H G N N A M E T K L P G H R T K F G R E
```

PAGE 22

```
        S                         N
G E N E S I S         S O N S
        F           S   P     A
        U           A B R A H A M
O L D       A       O       R
            C       M       K
    S               I
    H               S A R A H
B E L I E V E
    M
```

PAGE 24

```
H G T L S L A V E D V B C W A X S B M Q F
L D G B V C X Z W N A T I O N M B W Q G L
C H R R E B N M K P C Q W R T Y P M K G O
N B U V D N A T P C N M H B K L P K W B O
O X L D W Q S T M T P Y G E D W S Z Q R D
A F E T H W M Q B A R K T H G D S W Q S T
H G R B B Q V W N R Q G H G E N E S I S M
Y R T H G D C B M J O S E P H W G H M Q L
S G H K L A B R A H A M M R H P N I A R B
S P R B R H P R O M I S E Q T B T H L N T
```

PAGE 25

QUIZ 5

1. D
2. B
3. D
4. A
5. D
6. B
7. C
8. C

ANSWER KEY

PAGE 26

PAGE 28

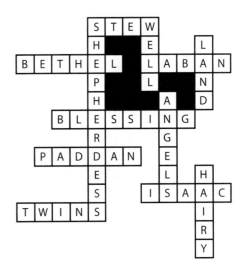

PAGE 29

QUIZ 6

1. A
2. C
3. D
4. C
5. B
6. C
7. B
8. C

PAGE 32

```
        A J V W K L E R G D
        Q S U Y L C M I H R S P
        S R T H G K L P T N B T S Q
        S R A T S G R N B E N J A M I N
      F N T L T W E L V E W F H A E L T P
    D R E B T R E U B E N S M Q M E T N T B
    G O T R D R E A M L T J N N D H N J W C
    Q B R O T H E R S H L T V S W B K L I W
    B E K L H P E S O J M W N T K N L S F R
    M P R I S O N T N N S R D H D N K E
      R S R K B I S R A E L W R P K M
        R R Y T J H F J T L B W N S
        T M U I L Z U Q M G A B
        V R A C B H Y F K O
```

177

ANSWER KEY

PAGE 33

QUIZ 7

1. C

2. C

3. B

4. C

5. C

6. D

7. B

8. C

PAGE 37

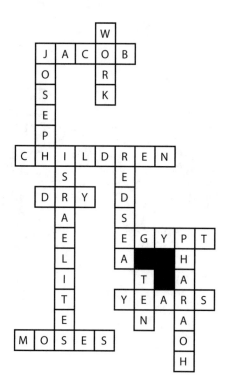

PAGE 38

```
K H M J Q Z C O M M A N D M E N T S
B O C A J M W N H F O R T Y N H G T
S G F H R M W Q R E D S E A Q R B T
H P E S O J S M T D T R E D A E L M
P Q N K P H A R A O H T S S B X N H
S D I S R A E L I T E S D W F S M Q
H E G Y P T I A N S N Q E X O D U S
C H R W I L D E R N E S S M H N O Q
```

PAGE 39

QUIZ 8:

1. B

2. D

3. C

4. D

5. A

6. C

7. A

8. B

PAGE 41

Crossword answers:
- THOUSAND
- ONE
- STONES
- SERVE
- SANG
- RAHAB
- DEW
- PROPHETESS
- ALTAR
- LORD
- PHRAIM
- MARCHED

PAGE 42

Word search grid:

```
P T T R U M P E T H D E B B H O D D
J T R H K D E B O R A H N R D S G B
O J O H C I R E J H M W A L L D B A
S B V I Y C A N A A N K L H N R N R
H C N T R I V E R W F R N B K D G M
U X S R E G D U J B D G H R S W C Y
A B N D M I D I A N B R V R W A Q T
N M K T G I D E O N T N A D R O J W
```

PAGE 44

QUIZ 9

1. C
2. A
3. C
4. B
5. C
6. D
7. A
8. D

PAGE 45

JOSHUA
ESTHER
DANIEL
NOAH
MOSES
ELIJAH
WIDOW

PAGE 46

LIONS

ANSWER KEY

PAGE 47

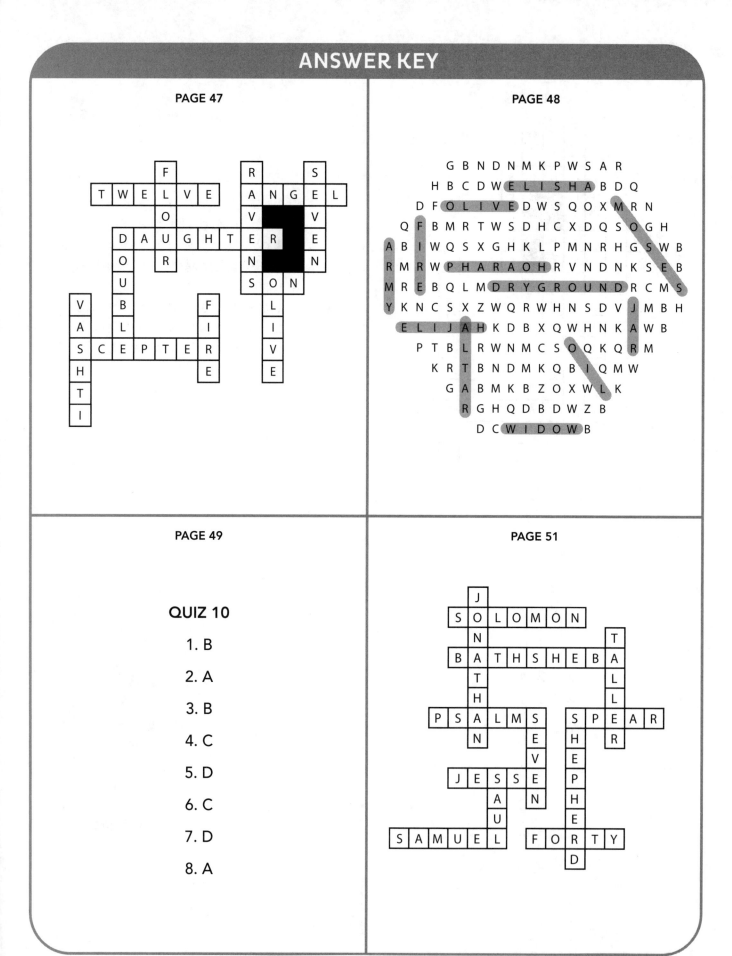

PAGE 48

PAGE 49

QUIZ 10

1. B

2. A

3. B

4. C

5. D

6. C

7. D

8. A

PAGE 51

PAGE 53

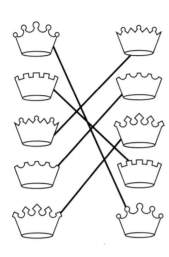

PAGE 54

"I have found David son of Jesse,
a man after my own heart;
he will do everything
I want him to do."

PAGE 56

GOLIATH

PAGE 57

QUIZ 11

1. D
2. C
3. C
4. B
5. D
6. A
7. C
8. B

PAGE 58

```
K M C Z Q R O N S R B S D B R HEART H K
R W H UNDERSTANDING K L N N T Y
D T C MODS I W C T F TRUST M L Y K N
ELBI B Q W P K Q PRAISE W D O M Q D
KNOWLEDGE T R P SHEPHERD G B
P D W Q G H S O E R T S P Q T S F W D H R W
W M D B Q PROVERBS F S T M Q R X C H
M B S B N T T D T H G BLESS W X C R N P
K L P W B R S C F W S D Q T Y D F X Z R M R
```

PAGE 59

PAGE 60

QUIZ 12

1. B

2. A

3. D

4. B

5. C

6. C

7. D

8. A

PAGE 62

PAGE 64

ANSWER KEY

PAGE 65

```
D N L D A N I E L M N S
J H D W H S I F K W Q C
E N L N L I O N S B D R
R H N B R F Y C S H G O
E W R K R E T T O P J L
M K B S D P R A Y H O L
I S M O U T H B F V N L
A W E E P I N G W N A P
H V N I N E V E H N H V
T R H S T A R S H I S H
```

PAGE 66

QUIZ 13

1. B

2. D

3. B

4. A

5. C

6. B

7. D

8. B

PAGE 67

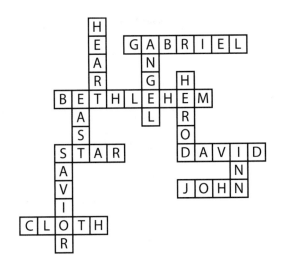

PAGE 69

```
R I M H M A R Y L P F V J E S U S B S G
T N C B E T H L E H E M S D B N S T T R
N D G Q S X Z S H E P H E R D S G A
B W I S E M E N N K E L B K T S D R
S D O R E H K N G J O S E P H S M M
N R O I V A S M E S S L E G N A
H E R D S R M A N G E R H O
```

ANSWER KEY

PAGE 70

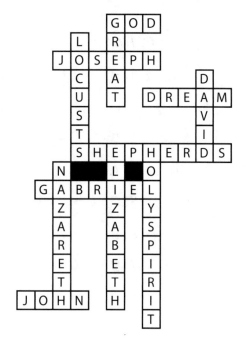

PAGE 72

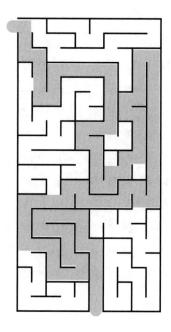

PAGE 73

```
K D S H E P H E R D S H M H B J
M H P P G K M P E E H S K R L O
A B R L T G A B R I E L M Q G H
R K N H S U S J E S U S W Q D N
Y N B C D L R J A N N A K L B
K N G L L E G N A V J L N P H R
S M S I M E O N K M J O S E P H
H T E B A Z I L E K Z D Z L W B
M S H S M E S S I A H K L T N D
```

PAGE 74

QUIZ 14

1. C
2. C
3. D
4. A
5. D
6. C
7. B
8. C

ANSWER KEY

PAGE 77

```
G H M D R E A M D R J E S U S
M Y H N R R H E R O D N K F T
Y S M T R A V E L C M B T H A
R B D S L E M A C M N T L S R
R E P O R T S W N L E G N A M
H R G H E A S T D H N B R S D
K L M K I N G N D G L N K L N
T V L R B M G O L D M N K B S
```

PAGE 78

PAGE 79

QUIZ 15

1. A
2. C
3. D
4. B
5. B
6. A
7. D
8. A

PAGE 81

MATTHEW and LUKE

PAGE 82

QUIZ 16

1. C
2. B
3. D
4. A
5. D
6. B
7. D
8. C

ANSWER KEY

PAGE 83

```
V O I C E N G
J O R D A N B S R T H
P R H M P R E P A R E K R H P
K M S S H A I S S E M N G R S
N H D O V E S R H N H O J N T
P S M P R I E S T N N A N N A
H E Z I T P A B N W A T E R W
M S S I M E O N K H M
T E M P L E G
```

PAGE 85

QUIZ 17

1. D
2. C
3. D
4. C
5. B
6. D
7. A
8. C

PAGE 86

SI_MO_N PE_T_ER

AN_D_R_E_W

J_A_M_E_S

J_O_H_N

P_H_I_L_I_P

BAR_TH_O_L_OM_EW

M_A_T_T_H_E_W

TH_O_MA_S

J_A_M_E_S
(son of Alphaeus)

SIM_O_N
(called the Zealot)

J_U_D_A_S
(son of James)

JUD_A_S IS_C_A_R_I_OT

PAGE 88

I WILL MAKE YOU

FISHERS OF MEN

PAGE 89

```
M       N           W           P
A       A     M     A   ANDREW   E
T     ISCARIOT  T           T
T       I     A     T           T   TWELVE
H       L     T     E           R   E
NETS    S     T     R   THUNDER  R
W             H           H
              I     JOHN  U
              A           N
              S     THREE  D
                          E
                          R
```

PAGE 90

HE H E A L S THE
    ★ ❄ ❀ ● ▲

B R O K E N H E A R T E D
❀ ❄ ▢ ❄ ❄ ■ ★ ❄ ❀ ❄ ▼ ❄ ❄

AND B I N D S UP THEIR
     ❀ ❄ ■ ❄ ▲

W O U N D S.
◗ ▢ ◆ ■ ❄ ▲

(Psalm 147:3 NIV)

PAGE 91

QUIZ 18

1. A

2. D

3. B

4. C

5. C

6. B

7. C

8. D

PAGE 93

PAGE 94

```
L K N D J A R S T R
C M L A C H K V J S R S
H S I F W V S N T O M B T H
N J D N G W N N X W A V E S
M R O T S C A H T B R K T L
Q N N A C R J T D B R E A D
K P S P E O P L E K H G B N
Z L A Z A R U S L R R T H M
V G N I D D E W L S V G
H G B A N A C Y S T
```

PAGE 95

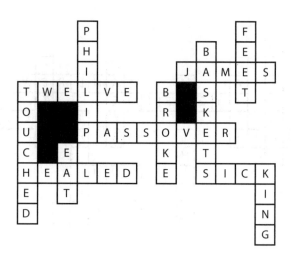

PAGE 96

PAGE 97

Jesus is the great healer.

PAGE 98

PAGE 99

QUIZ 19

1. C
2. A
3. B
4. C
5. D
6. A
7. C
8. D

PAGE 100

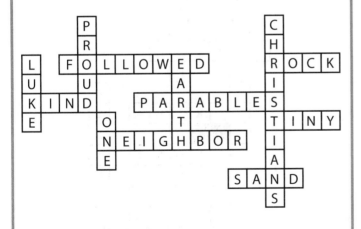

PAGE 101

C	O	M	E
✛	❑	○	❄

F	O	L	L	O	W
✦	❑	●	●	❑	◗

M	E
○	❄

ANSWER KEY

PAGE 103

```
                T
        B L E S S E D
    P U R E     A   T E A C H
        A       L   C I T Y
        T       T   H
    E N E M I E S
    A   T
    R   U
    T   D
    H   E   P E A C E
            S     R
          F     O
          A     W
        S T A N D
          H
          E
          R
```

PAGE 104

QUIZ 20

1. C

2. B

3. A

4. D

5. C

6. B

7. C

8. D

PAGE 105

PAGE 106

```
            W
        H O U S E
            R
    P       R
    E       I
  P R A Y E D
    F       D
    U
    M A R T H A       B
    E     H           E
    G L O R Y         L
          M           I
      F   A   L       E
      O   S T O N E   V
      U       V     D
    W R A P P E D
          D
```

PAGE 109

PAGE 110

```
    T L A S E
  M E R C Y C H
  B D E S S E L B T
M F C O M F O R T G D
C E A R T H D Y T I C A E
N B M O U N T A I N T H F C M
L I G H T N B P P E A C E P E J B
Q M H C A E T N B P L A M P E B A O H
N H B L H U M B L E T B L S S Z N T I J L
```

PAGE 113

QUIZ 21

1. A
2. C
3. D
4. B
5. B
6. D
7. C
8. A

PAGE 114

Our <u>FATHER</u> in heaven,

Hallowed be Your <u>NAME</u>.

Your <u>KINGDOM</u> come.

Your <u>WILL</u> be done

On <u>EARTH</u> as it is in <u>HEAVEN</u>.

Give us this day our daily <u>BREAD</u>.

And <u>FORGIVE</u> us our debts,

As we <u>FORGIVE</u> our debtors.

And do not lead us into temptation,

But deliver us from the <u>EVIL</u> one.

For Yours is the <u>KINGDOM</u> and the

<u>POWER</u> and the <u>GLORY</u> forever. Amen.

ANSWER KEY

PAGE 115

```
Q N E E D L W D T F G S R T
G H K M N B R E A D H Q K B D D
G B H Q W D S N M O D G N I K N A B
D F G W Q P R A Y E R B W M T L T I D B
N E V A E H H M R G R H D B K T X L T N
F M F O R G I V E W Q O M N K X T Y V T
D S R R O O D B C D W L N B G R W B X C
F A T H E R N B D Q Y Q E A R T H W
G T M V L R C K E E D N W S B M
N T E M P T A T I O N R S M
```

PAGE 118

QUIZ 22

1. D
2. B
3. C
4. D
5. C
6. D
7. A
8. C

PAGE 120

```
H M D G N I C O D E M U S N C M S L
Q R W R L T I G N I G H T Q K L N O
H G S H S I W E J N B T Y N S W T V
P W B E L I E V E M W N R O B H L E
B V N G A G A I N T H S A V E D K L
R S S R E D A E L M W Q S T O N S H
M D L P N S Q U E S T I O N S N G T
B V K L J E S U S N M W O R L D G F
```

PAGE 123

QUIZ 23

1. A
2. C
3. B
4. B
5. D
6. D
7. A
8. C

ANSWER KEY

PAGE 125

```
U B L A R H P J
Z E N O T S N M
R L Y J A S H E
N S I L V E R L
K E A R T H Q U A K E O T R Q K U H
P X G N S S O R C H M B T W I L M E
Y M C I H S O W N W L B E R Y K A J
L V P R I E S T S H U E L S N I T O
I T E O B A I F L E T R U T W S M C
Q S P A W O H G N Q R S F S H U T W
      B W O M E N J C
      C Z A N G E L I
      F D C R O W N T
      M H U B W O D S
      E Q G U A R D H
      X T O M B R L K
      H A N D W E G O
      V Y E P O K N W
      G D A R K L O M
      E J U S M R Q Y
```

PAGE 126

```
            P U R P L E
        G   I
        O   L
A L W A Y S   A T E
            B       G
T       G   A   A       L
H       O   T   B       I   J
F I V E H U N D R E D   A   O
R       H   A   B       L   S
S       A       B       E   E
T W O           B E L I E V E P
Y               A   O       E H
                S   R
                    D
```

PAGE 129

QUIZ 24

1. C
2. D
3. B
4. C
5. D
6. A
7. D
8. B

PAGE 131

193

ANSWER KEY

PAGE 133

```
        W D R H U
      O A M E N H G L K
    S T P E T E R D R O A D K
  V Q S D S A M O H T H L O V E
G H F I S H I N G T H L O C K E D
C L C L E O P A S K D L H B T K L
M S U A M M E T H A P P E A R H P
  K B R E A K F A S T K N B G R
    D O U B T K G R D T W D N
      J F D R F D C B N M P
        P J L E Y O I
```

PAGE 134

PAGE 135

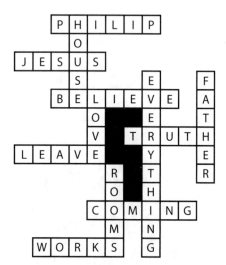

PAGE 136

QUIZ 25

1. B

2. C

3. A

4. D

5. B

6. C

7. D

8. C

ANSWER KEY

PAGE 137

```
D H K M R H T U R T S N V J E S U S Q W
G W K L D S Z W C B P O W E R T L S Z M
Q M I K N D S E M A L F M W H P T N T Q
B D H N Q W F R I E N D S D W O P L N V
D X C B D M K S P I R I T H W L L B V S
W B Q D I S C I P L E S W N Q B H Y N L
R E P L E H M K H C H R I S T I A N N B
M N B L A N G U A G E M W P T L J S Z Q
```

PAGE 138

The Holy Spirit is our helper.

PAGE 139

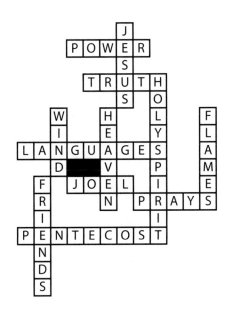

PAGE 141

```
    H C O M M A N D S G
P C B E C A E P K M W A Y N
R H P R P R E P A R E D M W
O H S K R O W T H N H Y B D
O T H F A T H E R G O G N R
M K C H T E A C H K U T H G
S M H E L P E R D Q S H N M
C M G N I M O C B R E C B W
D W Q H O L Y S P I R I T Q
```

195

ANSWER KEY

PAGE 142

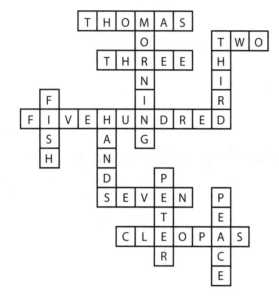

PAGE 143

QUIZ 26

1. D
2. C
3. A
4. C
5. B
6. D
7. C
8. B

PAGE 145

PAGE 146

27

PAGE 148

QUIZ 27

1. D
2. C
3. B
4. A
5. D
6. C
7. C
8. D

ANSWER KEY

PAGE 151

```
              F O R G I V E
              I     O
N E I G H B O R S   D
A           S     B
R       N O T H I N G   H
T       S     B     ■   E
C H R I S T   L O V E   A
    N         E         R
  U S                   T
```

PAGE 152

```
        I L O           K E L
      B E V J A        G O D S Q
    D V M I N D S      M C N T H L Y
  V D B T U H S A J    Y P H E A R T O E
  S C E V O L F R T H F M A O I R G U D S
  K R E A T S R K P K C H I L D R E N B N L H
  C Y M B A L F C W O B S A N H N B M T H H B
  X D S R O B H G I E N S M E R H K W C E X N
  O H C W I H D A E B O S G F O R E V E R M S
  N H C O M M A N D M E N T A H T R V C N
  R F S D W P L K J H G D S N K Q D B
    D R B E O I D S O U L T H P L O
    H Y H G B N T W D B N M T H
    H G B P A T I E N T D S
      B D R F A C H T B T
      W D N I K T H G
        C B N R T D
        R L W U
          C D
```

PAGE 155

QUIZ 28

1. C

2. B

3. A

4. C

5. A

6. D

7. B

8. D

PAGE 157

```
      F S R         N K L
    K F R U I T H G N L B
    G T S S E N D O O G H N B
    F R F A I T H F U L N E S S M
  H L W K V M L H K P E A C E N L K
  Y O J M G E N T L E N E S S M W Q
  K V Q N R F G N P A T I E N C E M
  S E L F C O N T R O L K N D J S N
  G H D K T N D N V T T J K O G
    T K I N D N E S S D V N Y
    H G B N L J E E R F Q
    N S P I R I T W S
```

ANSWER KEY

PAGE 158

```
        G O O D
        E
    L   N       P O W E R
  F A I T H     E
    W   L       A
      S E L F C O N T R O L
      P       E           O
      V I N E             V
      R           J       
      I         H O N E Y
      T         Y
```

PAGE 160

QUIZ 29

1. C
2. D
3. A
4. C
5. B
6. D
7. C
8. D

PAGE 161

```
        H G
      R D T K
    H S H A R E
    R L E T T E R S
    T Q N H C A E R P K
T H N G X R T C H R I S T I A N S K Q B
E N S S E N D L O B H Z N H N K M N V A
A R H D T C H C O R N E R S T O N E Q P
C B M I S S I O N A R Y N H I G R S N T
H T N R S H C R U H C W K T O S Q N C I
E Q T R H S D M Q D F R H M C H C V B Z
R H B O D Y O F C H R I S T H K H K T E
```

PAGE 163

QUIZ 30

1. C
2. D
3. D
4. B
5. D
6. D
7. A
8. A

198

ANSWER KEY

PAGE 164

```
E A S T
      R
C L O U D S
      M
A     P O W E R
N     E   H
L I G H T N I N G
E     T   I
L     T E A R
S         E
          W
      H   A
F O R E V E R D
      A   D
      V
      N E W
      N
```

PAGE 165

```
H N D W R T J E S U S T K S Z E Q N B W
Y A D E M O S L H T J C B R F A H R S A
K B V D R E T U R N H R T J R S K L M I
F A T H E R X N P H N E Z N J T D R B T
N B H D K N E V A E H L G Z F N J U N R
D M E V E R Y O N E N T B S Y P L L N T
M L E I K E Z E M W B P L Z F H N E V R
N D G H P R E P A R E K N W L T H N C T
N B H R D G C B K L R E V E L A T I O N
```

PAGE 166

QUIZ 31:

1. B

2. D

3. A

4. C

5. C

6. B

7. C

8. D

PAGE 167

```
    C J         I H
      A J L A C B O R D C K
    E A J Y A O D T Y E L P A J Y
    N I R O E V B U L A V E I R H S A
    M S U H S O O N D P E A W G U L K
    C U L S N L I E D T S L R O I H N E
    H E A V E N C W A N L A T B E G T
    I T N O H K E N O R H T B N Z R A
    N D S P A T M O S H I T I E N
      A W S G I L U M O M A A
      T R U M P E T N S R A
        C S A     H O L
```

199

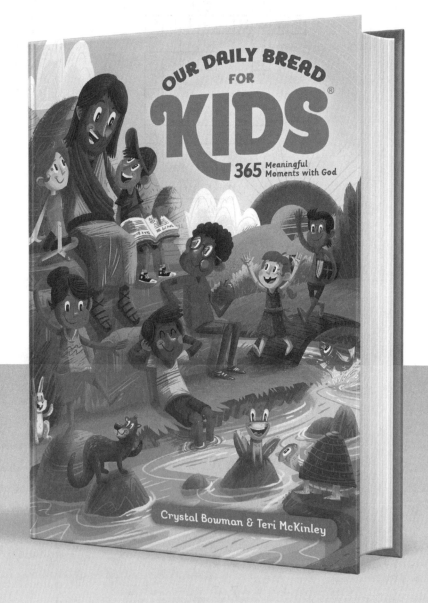